To
Babji, my grandpa and guardian angel
Mom & Dad for giving me this human experience
My godparents, Chenraj Uncle & Aunty
Cousin Jo, my niece and my nephew
Wendy Butterworth, who fought cancer till her last breath
May your light continue to guide us

Heal Your Gut, Mind & Emotions

5 Steps to Reset Your Health with Ayurveda and Food Chemistry

DIMPLE JANGDA

EBURY
PRESS

An imprint of Penguin Random House

EBURY PRESS

USA | Canada | UK | Ireland | Australia
New Zealand | India | South Africa | China | Singapore

Ebury Press is part of the Penguin Random House group of companies
whose addresses can be found at global.penguinrandomhouse.com

Published by Penguin Random House India Pvt. Ltd
4th Floor, Capital Tower 1, MG Road,
Gurugram 122 002, Haryana, India

First published in Ebury Press by Penguin Random House India 2023

10 9 8 7 6 5 4 3 2 1

ISBN 9780143463320

Typeset in Adobe Garamond Pro by Manipal Technologies Limited, Manipal

www.penguin.co.in

EBURY PRESS
HEAL YOUR GUT, MIND & EMOTIONS

Dimple Jangda has donned many hats before finding her calling in studies of gut health and Ayurveda. Her research in Ayurvedic science and food chemistry was based on her quest for good health.

She started Prana Healthcare Centre in 2017 with a team of Ayurvedic doctors, therapists and biotech researchers. Prana was featured as a case study by Routledge, Taylor & Francis publication, UK, in their book *Doing Business in South Asia*.

Dimple has received several honours, including Asia Iconic awards, Business World—Future Masters and Times Brand Icon 2021. She was recognized as '40 most influential under 40' by the Indian Achievers Club. Dimple also has also received honorary doctorates from The Thames International University in Paris and the National American University.

Her clinic and academy have helped patients and students from over sixty-four countries to recover from chronic diseases using Ayurveda and nutrition. She gives healthcare advice across various social media platforms, where half a million followers from over 100 countries have been tuning in every day.

Celebrating 35 Years of
Penguin Random House India

'This book serves as a captivating revelation, unravelling the enigma of the gut and its profound influence on the decisions we make about our health, both state of the mind and overall wellness. With insightful precision, it unveils the intricate connections between our gut, health and perceptive processes, urging us to retrace our roots, and embrace simple principles of Ayurveda and modern science to safeguard our holistic well-being'—Chenraj Roychand, chancellor, Jain University

'I met Dr Dimple at a time when I had a lot of stressors in my life. Needless to say, my gut health was at its worst. Simply put my experience with Dr Dimple has been life changing for my gut and therefore for my entire being. I feel lighter, happier and in control'—Waluscha De Sousa, actor

'Simple, impactful and to the point. Personally, I feel it's a perfect guide to perfect health'—Prabhu Nityanand Charan Das, bestselling author and practising monk

Contents

Foreword   ix
    by Juhi Chawla

Preface   xi

Introduction   xv

1. Understanding the Root Cause   1
2. It All Begins . . . in the Womb!   14
3. Unravelling the Mysteries of the Gut   28
4. 'I Have a Gut Feeling'   37
5. Your Unique Biological Blueprint   48
6. The Ayurvedic Energy Clock   79
7. Food Pyramid: Brickwork to Good Health   103
8. The Importance of Understanding the Digestion Period of Foods   126
9. Food Chemistry   136

10. Improve Your Relationship with Food   154
11. Seven Tools That Helped Shape My life . . . and
      Gut Health   167

Epilogue   189
Acknowledgements   193

Foreword

Juhi Chawla

The darkest hour of the night comes just before dawn.

Dimple's life is a classic example of how crisis can be a unique opportunity to change one's path, explore new opportunities and become the person one was meant to be.

From a childhood riddled with ill health and medications, an unhappy, abusive marriage and a cut-throat corporate position to a complete burnout, Dimple has lived it all, leading her to self-reflection and transformation. Today, she has become who she was meant to be, a torchbearer and a beacon of light.

Driven by passion and purpose, Dimple is determined to spread knowledge on health and well-being based on traditional Indian wisdom. Thanks to her media background, Dimple is an excellent speaker and teacher. Her clarity of thought and communication is remarkable.

Being an Indian, one inherently hears snippets on Ayurveda in their lifetime . . . *haldi doodh* and *kadhas* for cough and cold are a household affair. Having been educated in a modern school (where none of this wonderful wisdom is imparted), I was always confused about the relationship between Ayurveda and one's body. I heard elders saying, 'Ayurveda works slowly but has the power to heal completely, it works to cure the root of the problem.' Ayurvedic practitioners would be heard using words like '*vata, pitta, kapha*', but to the modern mind, most of this sounds like Greek and Latin, and to my mind, it was as Greek and Latin as Greek and Latin could be!

About three years ago during the lockdown, I found myself rather free, and out of curiosity, signed up for the 'Introductory Course to Ayurveda', which Dimple was conducting online. It truly turned out to be one of the best short courses I could have done. In two-hour sessions for five days, Dimple took us through the basic principles of Ayurveda so neatly and logically, directly relating them to the laws (or properties) of nature, that the foundational, basic concepts of Ayurveda became crystal clear. I find her book the same, full of good sense and powerful knowledge, backed by reason, she writes in a clear, crisp and riveting manner. I follow many of her tips based on Ayurveda, simply because, well, they are so sensible . . .!

When diet is wrong, medicine is of no use. When diet is correct, medicine is not needed.

In today's world of ever-increasing pressures and stresses of modern fast living, if one is interested in their own well-being and that of one's loved ones, we have to go back if we want to go forward. If one wants to bet on good health, rather than betting on good health insurance schemes then this book is a must-read. And not just once, but over and over again.

Juhi Chawla,
actor

Preface

Every time I look to the universe for answers, I almost always hear it say these exact same words: '*Trust your gut, and everything else will fall into place.*'

No matter the question I ask, I find my answer in this quote.

If you have been looking for answers on how to heal your body, mind and emotions from the irregularities of a modern lifestyle and the ravages of dysfunctional foods, or if you have been wondering how to improve the quality of your life and relationships, then you have arrived at the right place. The first step to our biological, intellectual and spiritual evolution involves having the hunger to grow and the curiosity to learn more. And you will be surprised to learn that the key to becoming the healthiest and kindest version of yourself, is already within you. It's your gut!

That's right.

Everything concerning your physical, mental and even emotional health begins and ends with the gut.

An entire universe has been placed inside you, complete with a trillion stars in the form of gut flora. This exhaustive collection of bacteria performs a variety of functions, including digestion, breaking down complex foods, aiding the absorption and assimilation of nutrients, eliminating toxins and even governing your mental make-up and emotional well-being! Like the 'God of small things', right now, your gut flora is giving a thumbs up to your decision to invest more time in your health. And by the way, that intuitive decision to pick up this book? It also came from your gut!

The healthier your gut, the healthier your overall physical, mental and emotional health will be. Your gut is like the fuel engine that provides nutrients for all your other organs, and it was designed by the finest engineer in this universe—Mother Nature herself. She had a wild imagination and an ambitious plan when she challenged herself to pack so many miracles into a human body. A tiny egg and sperm fuse to create a marvellous human being, fitted with a complex set of organs that are crafted to perfection. A tiny heart that beats every single moment from the time it is forged in the uterus until the last breath; a brain that processes complex information at lightning speed; and the gut force of a trillion bacteria working tirelessly to convert nutrients inside this human body!

Mother Nature packed in several other miracles too—in the form of the stomach, gall bladder, liver, kidneys, intestines and limbs, replete with pinkie toes and fingers in five unique sizes; eyes that can consume ten million bits of information per second and perceive the magic of this universe; ears that can convert sound into deep, spiritual meaning; a nose that can sense trouble as well as delicious food; and a mouth that speaks many tongues, most importantly, the language of humanity and kindness.

As an epilogue to this grand theatrical production, she infused the breath of life into this body in the form of deep, rich scarlet blood circulating through our veins, and wrapped this divine being in several layers of muscle and delicate skin that is continuously breathing and growing. Her final stroke was the most brilliant one: she gave this body a spirit that is ageless, timeless, genderless and full of wisdom. No man-made modern technology could ever compete with this masterpiece.

If you are not a miracle, then what is? If you ever need a boost of confidence, remind yourself that you are the sum of all the magical things that have happened in this universe for you to exist at this exact moment in time. This human experience is a special gift. Guard it safely, protect it, nourish it and express gratitude to your parents, Mother Nature and this body for allowing you this human experience.

* * *

In this book, I am going to share with you the tools that shaped my life, the mysteries of the gut, a 5000-year-old, time-tested, ancient Ayurvedic science, the magical healing remedies from your kitchen, and how you can use food to preserve your health and reverse diseases. Together, we will learn how to unlock the huge potential of the gut using a five-step process and improve our gut–brain axis so it can share critical information with us on what the body truly needs.

These tools are backed by modern evidence-based science, which will also appeal to your rational intelligence. But remember this: Nature created humanity, and humanity created science to understand the mysteries of this universe and the power of nature. Any science that takes you closer to nature, your source energy and your creator, will remain the most authentic of all sciences. Everything else is a symptomatic approach without addressing the root cause. Most importantly, allow these tools and insights to appeal to your intuitive intelligence, which is a natural software, a GPS that Mother Nature installed within you for survival, to navigate through this world and improve the quality of your life. So read with an open mind, be ready to unlearn old habits that no longer serve you and build new health habits that can potentially reset your gut and your life.

As you flip through these pages, discovering secrets about your body, remember the butterfly effect.

Just as the flapping of a butterfly's wings in one part of the world can alter the course of a typhoon halfway across the world, a small shift in your habits can move the needle on your health compass and forever change your path and thus your destination!

Introduction

God Is in the Details

At the age of sixteen, I had a cancer scare.

I detected a tumour in my body, but I didn't tell my mother about it for the longest time because I thought I was going to die.

Soon after, I struggled to breathe, and the ache became unbearable. I had to inform my mother and we rushed to the hospital. What followed was painful needle biopsies, scans and radiation from mammograms, which left me traumatized for several years. Luckily for me, the cyst was benign, but it became highly fibrocystic from the radiation and grew to the size of my fist. Within two weeks, I had to undergo surgery, and they found four more tumours. When I went to get my stitches removed, they found a new tumour. A year later, one more surgery.

By the age of eighteen, I had undergone four surgeries for fibrocystic benign tumours, inflamed tonsils and a deviated septum. It was a new record in my family! I remember waking up during one of those surgeries and feeling like I was trapped inside a paralysed body. I could hear the doctors and nurses talking, but I couldn't move my body. I screamed inside my head, hoping they would hear me. That nightmare returned years later to haunt me when I was deep-sea diving in Bali. My ears got blocked, and I started to hallucinate, became motionless and saw the surgery scene as if it were happening right there, underwater. It was an eerie déjà vu—the same feeling of being trapped in my own physical body. I learned that:

> *Your body does not forget the trauma of surgery for*
> *seven years.*

Your physical, mental, emotional and energetic body carries memories of the surgery even years after the scars have faded. It doesn't forget. In fact, our bodies carry memories of the diseases that our ancestors have been through and of human evolution itself on a cellular level. We inherit these memories and natural fears in our DNA, lock them in different parts of our bodies, and they can get triggered by the wrong lifestyle and food habits and manifest as diseases. I was deeply scarred by my sickness at many levels, and this event had a cascading negative effect on all aspects of my life. My body confidence hit a new low; my skin, hair, body posture and ability to heal suffered; and my intuitive intelligence, or gut feeling and ability to make good decisions in life were broken.

My extended family was undergoing similar health crises. We lost an uncle to depression and suicide, leaving behind three children still in school. My cousins were traumatized for several years. That's the impact of suicide on people. It's the family, friends and relatives left behind that feel the impact of this decision for the rest of their lives. Mental health was not something that was spoken about in our community back then, and the social stigma didn't make it easy for those suffering either.

Two years later, another uncle succumbed to depression and a sudden heart attack. Four weeks later, my father was hospitalized for a critical open-heart surgery to rid of multiple blockages. The doctors were surprised that he hadn't succumbed to a heart attack earlier. He battled for his life, wrote his will and prepared us for the worst. He kept his surgery a secret from his mother so as not to add to her suffering. Tragically, three days after my father's open-heart surgery, his mother died of a heart attack. Her heart was broken from the loss of her two sons, and she could not see her favourite son before taking her last breath. At the funeral, I was all by myself, handling a tornado of inquiries from distant relatives asking why my father had failed to show up. My job was to keep them away from the hospital so they wouldn't break the news of his mother's death to him. A few days later, when my father returned from the ICU, we told him that his mother was no more. It felt like a curse. Suddenly, our entire family was under a dark cloud of death and disease.

All of us were shattered and still reeling under the shock, unable to even cry. I wanted to do anything I could to lift this curse off my family and end this series of deaths. When my father returned from the hospital, he had lost his will to live. He wanted to quickly get us married. Being the eldest daughter, I felt it was my duty to shoulder the responsibility. He brought a family home on a recommendation, and after two meetings, I agreed to marry a complete stranger at the age of twenty-one. I thought my decision would give my father a reason to live and a few years of joy.

The wedding date was rushed, and I was to be married within two months. But the days leading up to the wedding were filled with catastrophic events and messages from the universe asking me to walk away. I wish I had listened to my gut. I was in a car accident outside my home, barely fifteen minutes before I met this man for the first time. The car was damaged, but we were fine. On the day of the engagement, my car was towed, and I was delayed for my ceremony. My aunt and uncle were caught in a rigamarole as they missed their train and boarded the wrong train twice. It was hard to understand why so many mishaps were happening on the same day. Two weeks before my wedding, I developed a strange fever—it was neither dengue nor malaria. But I had it for several days leading up to the wedding and even after. I was scared and felt alone . . . like a goat about to be sacrificed. Nothing made sense or felt right. But I kept convincing myself that everything would work out in the end.

I was naïve and believed everyone in this world was a kind human being. What I did not expect was a near-death experience in an abusive marriage. On the first day of being married, my in-laws took stock of everything—my jewellery, cash, wedding gifts and electronics. My ex-husband wanted to sell all my jewellery to buy land in his name. When I refused, the torture started. He changed my phone number, and thereafter, all my calls and messages were monitored. I subtly asked my parents to stop giving me any more gifts. He was enraged and started punishing me. I would do all the cooking for a family of seven; the maids never lasted. One maid even tried to commit suicide in our kitchen one morning. My brother-in-law found her choking and hanging from the ceiling fan, and he quickly brought her down. My father arranged for her a safe trip back home. She said she was tired of my mother-in-law picking on her all day.

The abuse continued. I didn't let him come anywhere near me. Every day, he would find new ways to threaten me and break my spirit. Once, he threatened to divorce me, and another day, he verbally abused my dark skin. He said he felt sorry for my father's health and that I was jeopardizing my brother's and sister's futures with my behaviour. Some days, he would talk about wife-swapping clubs. He would suddenly cry loudly, asking me to take care of him. And the next day, he would tell me stories of how a woman jumped off the terrace after twenty years of marriage. He would repeatedly ask me why my uncle had killed himself. Another day, he and his mother started to push me around and threatened to beat me if I didn't cooperate. There was milk boiling in the kitchen. I told myself not to talk back or agitate them further. There was already a woman in their family whose body was charred from an 'accident' involving hot oil. One wrong turn and my life could be over in a minute.

There was dowry harassment, mental, emotional and verbal abuse, manipulation and gaslighting when I refused to give him my inheritance or ask my family for more. I was frightened of him. I had no communication with my friends, and I couldn't tell my parents either, as I was afraid it would affect my father's health. I kept a diary of the daily abuse. He found it, accused me of scheming against him and destroyed it.

I was not allowed to talk to the neighbours or go out on my own, even to the vegetable market. I was always accompanied by his mother or his sister to make sure I didn't speak to anyone.

I prepared for my fourth-grade exam in violin and continued my kathak classes to keep me distracted. My violin teacher had helped me buy an antique 300-year-old Antonio Stradivari violin before my marriage, and it was very dear to my heart. But I was forced to discontinue music and dance lessons. My ex-husband gave my music system to his brother and my violin to his sister. My violin teacher sensed that something was wrong and agreed to come home to teach music to this man's sister, just so he could check up on me. I was silenced like a lamb as I watched them play the violin. After this incident, I never played music again.

I had to find something else to keep me sane, to keep me calm. They were constantly trying to convince me that I had a problem. I asked the universe for help and the one friend who was able to get through me introduced me to meditation. I would wake up at 4 a.m., take a cold shower, sit on the terrace and meditate. Some days, I would close my eyes and open them again to find that two hours had passed in a blink with zero thoughts. Some days, the fear took over my mind and flooded it with so many dark thoughts that I would freeze. Every day was a challenge, and I was afraid for my life.

The universe sent me music. My brother-in-law noticed I was lonely and gave me a small iPod the size of two of my fingers, with the Buddha Bar albums VI and VII loaded in it. During the day, I worked in the kitchen for seven to eight hours. When I had time to rest, I would close my eyes and listen to this music. I allowed the music to take me to faraway lands where there was no fear, no worry and no pain, but only bliss and solitude. Those moments were deep and meditative, when time stood still, and the physical limitations of my body didn't exist. My soul was free to travel, and I was teleported into a parallel universe. Sometimes, I was in the middle of a desert, all alone under the moonlight, surrounded only by music, and sometimes, I was in the mountains. I felt and heard nothing else outside of this state. One day, my sister-in-law called out to me, and I didn't budge. She shook me vigorously to wake me out of this meditative state. What I had experienced was bliss and unconditional joy. I couldn't feel any anger or hate inside of me for anyone at that moment. It was like experiencing the heavens, the gods, the infinite stretch of this universe and the brilliance of a million stars. It was beautiful and surreal. I held on to this feeling to help me navigate through the dark days.

Meditation and music saved my life. I became very aware of my surroundings. When my ex-husband would return home from work, I would stop ironing clothes, and put the clothes iron in a safe zone. I avoided going to the terrace or balcony when he was around, and I wouldn't heat oils or milk in his presence. I hid all the cooking fuels in the house. I stayed calm and watched my back at all times. He allowed me to paint, and I made a life-size artwork of a geisha; her lips were sealed, but her eyes spoke volumes of her struggles.

At night, I would curl up in a foetal position, ready to defend myself and pray to God, 'Watch over me if I fall asleep. I want to live to tell my story.'

I was trapped in a coffin. I tried to leave twice but was convinced to return to my marriage. During the last few days of my marriage, I was held hostage with no access to a phone. He threatened consequences for my siblings' future if I tried to speak against him. Meanwhile, behind my back, he started approaching my relatives, neighbours and family without my knowledge and convinced them that I was suffering from hallucinations and had suicidal tendencies, and that only he could take care of me.

One night, I managed to make a phone call to my grandfather. The very next day, my parents were sent to rescue me, but they were also held hostage and not allowed to leave. After several hours of convincing them that I would return, we left with just the clothes I was wearing and a small purse with keys that opened no more doors.

I was under a lot of pressure from my ex-husband, society, neighbours and relatives who formed a kangaroo court, asking me to return to my marriage. Society frowned upon me, saying I was setting a bad example for other girls who silently suffered in their marriages. I lost faith in humanity.

My grandfather took me to Bengaluru. I was so shaken that I couldn't speak.

My uncle asked me to write down everything that had happened—it ran up to forty-eight pages. I relived the nightmare as I wrote it down. I had developed such severe insomnia that I barely slept for an hour each day. My uncle enrolled me in yoga classes, after which I was able to sleep for an extra hour due to exhaustion. He asked me to start painting, and so I did. I made a large painting of Sai Baba, his spiritual guide, which looked lifelike, the eyes glistening in the dark due to the oils. When my aunt walked past it early one morning, she jumped, thinking Sai Baba was sitting there. My uncle gave that artwork the highest place in his home, and he prayed to it every day. That day marked the beginning of my new life.

After some months of battle, I was free of the marriage. But it took me many years to heal my broken heart and learn to trust again.

Every single day, thousands of women around the world are sacrificed on society's altar for greed, dowry, lust and patriarchy, undergoing on a daily basis gaslighting, manipulation, toxic chauvinism, societal and government oppression, physical, mental, verbal, emotional and sexual abuse, sometimes within the safety of their own homes and marriages. Every woman is Nirbhaya and Mahsa Amini. She carries in her soul all their stories.

But let me emphasize that this is not a sob story. Look closely, and you will notice an obvious pattern and the root cause of the tragic events in my life: it all started with the lack of good health and the many diseases in my family. Remember:

Your health has a domino effect on
all aspects of your life and your loved one's life!

When the chips fall, it will not be in your favour. And to pick up your life again from those pieces and reverse diseases is the hardest thing you will have to do. Which is why it is easier to preserve health than cure disease. Your health and nutrition are your responsibility alone. Not the responsibility of doctors, nutritionists, healers, astrologers or the pharma companies! You are in charge of this body. Your body is a gift from Mother Nature, and you must care for it, nourish it and use it wisely.

The best gift you can give your loved ones,
is by existing in good health!

Life insurance is good for security. But if you could invest even a small fraction of that money in preventive healthcare, you will live a healthy life today and tomorrow.

When I moved to Bengaluru, my grandfather became my best friend. I shared all my stories and the day's events with him. He had the wisest things to say, and some of them were radical ideas that involved breaking social stereotypes boldly and unapologetically. My uncle was a godfather to me. He was a one-of-a-kind, progressive man and the founder of Jain (deemed-to-be) University, a group of eighty-five schools and colleges. He strongly believed that only education could dispel the evils of society.

I did my master's in international business and worked two jobs while still in college. I became a TV reporter with a local news channel and went to college in the evenings. Then I moved to Mumbai for a TV producer role (I was given a massive promotion—from intern to TV producer, without a hike in my salary!), and returned to college on the weekend to take my exams. During this time, my insomnia was a boon. It helped me juggle work and studies. I completed my post-graduation with a gold medal and a couple of awards at national-level college festivals.

When I worked in television, I practically worked around the clock. I woke up at 3.30 a.m. every single day and went to work by 4 a.m. to start production for the first live show of the day on stock markets. I stayed until late in the evening and even worked on weekends to improve my skills. I never saw the sun rise or set for a whole year. It broke my back. Vitamin D deficiency caused my spinal cord to become weaker, and I ended up with a prolapsed disc. My time at CNBC-TV18 taught me that you cannot trade your health for wealth or success in your career. *Health is not a chip for barter.* I learned a valuable lesson. No matter who we think we are:

> *We are nothing but a houseplant with complex emotions.*
> *We need three basic things for survival—sunlight, water*
> *and nutrients to grow.*
> *Love is a bonus.*

When I felt saturated at work and didn't find enough growth opportunities, I took a sabbatical to study finance and reinvent my career in investment banking. I worked with two boutique firms and learned the ropes of the trade. But the desk job and poor posture worsened my spinal health. One day, the disc prolapsed, and I was screaming in pain in the office. My colleague rushed me to the hospital. Another time, in the middle of a dance floor at a friend's reunion party, my disc prolapsed again, and I froze right there. The next day, I was flown home to my parents, where I was bedridden for two months. I spent days and nights staring at the ceiling, feeling helpless and depressed. I thought my life was over. I promised God that I would stop dancing and staying out late if he fixed me since I had no other vice to give up as a bribe.

The darkest hour comes before the sun rises

I took the time to do yoga, physiotherapy, meditate and chant to undo all the damage. When I recovered, my life took a sudden turn. I received an offer to head a cross-border mergers and acquisitions transaction in the Indian BOT toll roads and hydropower sector and pitch it to potential buyers on Wall Street.

Life was good again. I lived in New York and would fly to Chicago for work. I travelled to many countries and checked all the places off my bucket list.

I enjoyed my work, the power game and the mad adrenaline rush that came with it.

Then came autumn. The chilly winds started to creep into my heart, whispering strange things. By winter, I was frozen from the inside. I couldn't feel anything. On the eve of Christmas, I woke up in my hotel room feeling lifeless and numb. The cold was seeping into my bones, and it felt like I was consumed by an ever-growing dark cloud.

I didn't know what it was then. Was it the Chicago weather or depression? I know now that I was undergoing a severe existential crisis and depression symptoms from it. I lived a luxurious materialistic life lacking purpose and meaning. My spirit was wounded by the many past events of my life, and I never took the time to heal. I had mastered the art of suppressing my emotions, putting them all in boxes and stacking them away in the dark corners of my heart so I wouldn't have to deal with them. Suddenly, all of my past demons resurfaced. And I had nowhere to hide.

Tragic moments in our lives make a lasting impact. They are strong memories that we carry all our lives like a burden on our shoulders or a thorn in our flesh. We may not see them, but they continue to grow stronger by the day, feeding on our good energies, vibrations and nutrition. They become stronger and thicker, like spikes in our flesh. Over the years, we collect more spikes and begin to resemble a figurative porcupine. Defensive, alone and scared.

Depression is not the hardest part. It is recognizing that you are in pain and doing the healing work that is the toughest.

All my life's events flashed before my eyes. The ailments, the surgeries, losing family members, the abusive marriage, being held hostage, getting disowned by society and living in flight mode since then. Surely there was a reason for my sufferings? Because:

The Universe doesn't make mistakes.

The irony of the situation was that, exactly seven years ago, during Christmas, my parents had rescued me from a hostage situation. Fast forward to seven years later, I was living in the Garden of Eden as Satan hissed in my ears, tempting me to stay in this luxurious world. Or I could walk away into the dark, into an unknown abyss, hoping to find myself again.

Was it a dream or was I waking up?

I knew I had to do something to save myself from this overwhelming darkness and this sinking ship. I decided to take a leap of faith, packed my bags, stored them away in NYC, and returned to India to find answers. I was on an indefinite sabbatical.

In my many prayers before, I had made bucket lists, and the universe granted every single wish on them. When I was twenty, I wrote that I wanted to get an MBA, live in New York and start my own business. But shortly after, I got married and I forgot about the list or my dreams. Suddenly, two years later, a tornado hit my life, uprooted me completely, destroyed everything in its path and made my bucket list come true.

This time around, I didn't know what I wanted. I had lived a good life so far. And I was lucky to be alive. Instead of making a new bucket list or manifesting, I spoke to the universe, saying, 'Tell me what you want! What is the purpose of my existence? And I will work towards making it come true. Give me a reason to wake up.'

I allowed the Universe to guide me. I flowed with the current of the river. It was both scary and liberating at the same time. I learned a powerful lesson:

The most stressful situations in life require you to be the calmest.

Imagine you were looking for a diamond ring that fell into a lake. If you become anxious and move frantically, there will be more ripples in the water, the sand beneath will rise, and the water will become murky. But if you stay very still, the lake will become placid, and you will be able to see clearly. You will find what you lost—the ring or your purpose in life.

Embrace the moment, and let it pass.

I returned to India and received invitations from banks to consider some distressed assets for the acquisition. In between factory visits, I would explore the countryside of all the cities I went to: Jaipur, Udaipur, Bhavnagar, Bhuj, Chennai, Mamallapuram, Davanagere and Bengaluru.

I would spend at least two months analysing and determining the financial feasibility of each project. And on the D-Day of decision making, I would ask myself, 'Will I be excited to wake up in the morning and manufacture cutting tools in France, run a hotel in Jaipur or head a packaging company in Mumbai?' When I didn't feel it in the gut, I dropped the business model, unattached to the amount of time and work that had already been spent on it and moved on to my next project. I was looking for the spark that could light my spirit—something that my Gods would be proud of me doing. This search continued for two years, and I was living off my savings. Had the universe told me that it would take me two years to find my purpose, I would have probably taken up one of those corporate offers and made some decent money. But because of the uncertainty of what I was looking for, I continued to be spontaneous with my decisions. After all:

The universe speaks to you through serendipity.

In the countryside, I interacted with the locals, the shepherds and the farmers. I visited ancient temple ruins and explored local history, heritage, culture and food.

I saw that, in the countryside, joy and unconditional happiness seemed like an everyday normal. It was not a phenomenon, but something normal. People were naturally in a state of kindness and self-love and in tune with the rhythm of Mother Nature. I was beginning to experience unconditional happiness too. For the first time, it was happiness without a reason or excuse. Just happiness.

Something inside me started to shift. I was smiling more often and sleeping deeply for the first time in years. My chronic insomnia and fear of falling asleep were gone, just like that. I slept like a baby and woke up refreshed and hungry. I was energetic and had a voracious appetite for someone who hated food as a child. For a petite person, I was able to wipe an entire thali clean, much to the wonder of the waiters. Something magical was happening inside of me. I rhythmically woke up with the sun and would retire with the sun; my internal clock was in sync with Mother Nature. For the first time, my life didn't run by the clock or the calendar but responded to Mother Nature!

Such a joy to be born again

It was like a rebirth. I could feel the happiness and peace sink into my bones.

Simple joys such as watching the clouds pass over the moon or the sheep grazing, having conversations with a random stranger in a village and taking in the smell of the earth while walking amidst tall trees were suddenly the most precious moments of my life. Happiness was simply being able to be in the moment. It was pure and unconditional, like the joy on a newborn's face when looking at its mother.

During one such road trip, from Udaipur to the royal palace in Bhavnagar for a meeting, I had a life-changing, epiphanous moment.

I met a shepherd who did not wear a watch, but he could tell the time of the day simply by looking at the sky; that is how he could figure out what the weather would be like as well. And despite the rugged life and lack of luxuries, he was the happiest man I'd met. The shepherd and I spoke briefly. I asked him about his village, his work and then a rather silly question: 'Are you content with life?' His answer was everything I needed to hear at that moment. He said, 'Why not? I have good work, the sun and clean air, and I am going home for dinner now.'

Happiness was so simple and easy, without condition, without reason, without a necessary romantic explanation or theory. It was just . . . happiness.

I had a grand plan right then and there. I decided, 'I am going to sell happiness.' I would bottle this unconditional happiness and become a millionaire. I started putting together a 'happiness project', complete with details of land parcels that I identified on several trips, a financial model with yearly projections, a profit and loss statement, an investors' pitch, team details and a feasibility report with details on the economy, the market size, potential clients and their profiling in terms of age, nationality and needs. The project was based on the concept of 'going back to nature', and included sciences such as Ayurveda, naturopathy, acupuncture, yoga, meditation, pottery, organic farming and horse therapy for post-traumatic stress disorders (PTSD).

Health and happiness are synonymous. If you are healthy, you experience happiness. And when you are happy, your body responds to that happiness at a cellular, physical, mental and emotional level.

Nature creates, and nature heals

I met with one of the oldest families of Ayurveda—Vaidyaratnam Oushadhasala, who are also ashta vaidyas, an ancient terminology for one who has mastered the eight branches of Ayurveda. They were also one of the remaining eight families that received this wisdom from Parashurama 5000 years ago and carried this legacy forward.

Initially, the clinic, Prana Healthcare Centre, was set up as a corporate social responsibility initiative, a way for me to give back to society. I had no intention to study Ayurveda and planned to remain behind the scenes. But I noticed a huge communication gap between doctors and patients, and between modern lifestyles and traditional medicines. There was a language gap, a lifestyle gap and a research gap. In an attempt to bridge this gap, I spent the next few years researching and studying, looking for answers. And I became an accidental health coach.

The team grew, and we brought on board interns with backgrounds in biotechnology, forensic science and gut microbiome research. We married modern research-based science with traditional Ayurvedic science in an effort to understand the root cause of diseases. Since its inception, patients from over fifty-four countries have visited the clinic and received Ayurvedic therapies for post-cancer chemotherapy detox, bronchial diseases, neurological disorders, gastrointestinal disorders, gynaecological diseases, skin diseases, musculoskeletal disorders, psychosomatic imbalances and other issues.

Along with Ayurvedic panchakarma, we introduced nutrition, lifestyle change advice and counselling sessions to address emotional issues and avoid relapses. The clinic became a pivot point where people visited, experienced epiphanies and found answers within. Life would never be the same again for them. The clinic became a *kalpavriksh*, or a wishing tree, where your wishes could come true.

Decoding a 5000-year-old natural science that has withstood the test of time and humanity and making it a global phenomenon and a household practice became the vision and purpose of our clinic. We found our way to understanding gut health. And the whole time, I could hear the universe saying to me:

'Trust your gut and everything will fall into place.'

1

Understanding the Root Cause

When we were kids, my sister and I got our tonsils removed on the same day. I was afraid of needles and hospitals even back then and disappeared into a neighbour's room when the nurse appeared with a syringe. I kept shouting and kicking even as they tried to introduce anaesthesia. Looking back, it was an unnecessary surgery. The inflammation in the tonsils was caused by foods such as sugar, dairy and ice-cream, and could have been treated without surgery. At Prana, we have been able to avoid surgeries for children by introducing them to potent anti-inflammatory foods, such as honey, holy basil, pepper and ginger, to boost their immunity and overall health. There are also Ayurvedic medicines such as chyawanprash (Indian gooseberry jam), suvarnaprashan drops and saraswatarishtam, which is made with herbs like vachca (acoraceae), shanka pushpi (convolvulus pluricaulis choisy), brahmi (Indian pennywort), guduchi satva (giloy or tinospora cordifolia), yashti (liquorice), ashwagandha (Indian ginseng), ghee (clarified butter) and ash of purified gold. These herbs help improve a child's physical strength, stamina, immunity, brain development, memory power and intellectual power. It allows the child to build immunity to fight the inflammation inside instead of resorting to extreme measures like surgery and drugs.

My experience with fibroids and cysts made me understand that the root cause lay in my choice of foods and the skincare products I used. The doctors kept prescribing surgeries, but nobody could guarantee that the cysts wouldn't come back. I was advised to undergo a fifth surgery, which I flatly refused. I figured that the root cause of my cysts was excess oestrogen in my body from a heavy diet of dairy and soya products that I was put on earlier. As a teenager, I was addicted to roll-on deodorants, and many years later, I realized that the aluminium in them gets absorbed through the sweat pores and deposits itself in the breast tissue, causing cysts and fibroids in women and men. Even men can get breast cancer.

I decided to change my diet and lifestyle and remove all hormonal foods that trigger the production of oestrogen. I was already a vegetarian—meat, seafood and eggs were never part of our diet, thanks to our cultural background. I also stopped eating other foods that cause oestrogen to rise, such as soya, tofu, edamame, tempeh, peaches, dates, prunes, pumpkin seeds, flax seeds, sesame seeds and garlic; dairy products such as milk, yoghurt, buttermilk and cheese; berries, wheat bran and cruciferous vegetables such as cabbage and cauliflower. I was advised to simply apply warm castor oil to the cyst. It started shrinking. I also noticed that when I had a good sleep cycle, exercised well and was in stress-free natural environments with clean air, my cyst would shrink. But when I was back in the city, got stressed, didn't exercise or didn't pay attention to my diet, the cyst would grow. It was like a warning bulb placed inside of me, shrinking or growing to ensure I stayed on track. As my gut health, digestion and metabolism improved, I was able to avoid the fifth surgery.

After several years, I also understood the root cause of repeated fibroids in my uterus, sinusitis issues and the resulting deviated septum surgery. Someone had wrongly advised me to go on a diet of soya milk, which not only impaired my digestion but also caused my sinuses to get inflamed and heavily blocked. The doctors didn't explain the root cause or give us an alternative healthcare solution; they simply put me under the knife again. It was the most painful surgery. I woke up with my nose plastered; dried blood filled my throat and I couldn't breathe or swallow food and water for days while my nose continued to bleed. My head spun at the sight of blood.

At Prana, we meet several patients who are advised deviated septum surgery to treat their sinusitis. Instead, we offer them a simple Ayurvedic therapy called *nasyam*, in which—based on their unique body type and symptoms—medicated oils such as anu thailam, bala thailam, kukumadi thailam or ghee are introduced through the nostrils for seven consecutive days. These medicated oils reduce inflammation and flush out the mucus from the sinus passage. Nasyam also helps stimulate the nerve fibres in the nose bridge, which are directly connected to the pituitary gland. This not only treats the sinuses but also balances hormones; manages symptoms of Parkinson's disease and Alzheimer's; treats neurological disorders, anxiety, stress, depression and insomnia; and even helps lighten dark circles and pigmentation on the skin. It is one of the five detoxification methods available in Ayurveda that can be done at home. This treatment alone has helped several of our patients avoid surgery and recover naturally.

A diet protocol is also prescribed where all inflammatory foods, including dairy products, gluten, meat, carbonated drinks, cold water and ice cream, are eliminated. They are replaced with warming foods such as honey, ginger, pepper, turmeric, cinnamon and warm water all day, which help liquify the mucus. Another trick that helped me heal my sinusitis was steam inhalation with a few drops of eucalyptus oil, which is anti-inflammatory. It eases breathing and also reduces cold sores, blood pressure, blood sugar and fever symptoms.

You can also take three to four teaspoons of ajwain (carom seeds), dry roast them on a pan and place them inside a small handkerchief. Make a poultice bag out of it and inhale it slowly through both nostrils. This helps reduce the pressure and inflammation in the sinus areas. You can also massage your temple to reduce the pressure on your sinuses.

Another delicious remedy is to boil ginger with some mint leaves in a glass of water and sip it when it is warm. For frequent sneezing bouts, take four black peppercorns and chew on them slowly. This helps kill the bacteria in the mouth and bronchial region. You can also do *jal neti*, a yoga practice of flushing the sinus passages with warm water and salt through one nostril and letting it flow out through the other nostril. After nasyam and jal neti, always remember to gargle with warm water, turmeric and salt to prevent parasites from irritating the throat.

Make sure your sinus passages are always clear, as the accumulated bacteria and mucus can block your ear canals and affect your eyesight too.

If you have been struggling with blocked ears or earaches, Ayurveda suggests *karnapurana*, an effective remedy that introduces medicinal oils through the ear canal. Once, a young mother who felt she was losing her hearing flew down from New York to Mumbai for this treatment, and for the first time in several years, her ears popped open and she started recovering. What you can do at home is warm a few drops of sesame oil indirectly by placing the oil bottle in a bowl of hot water. Place your pinkie finger for five to ten seconds in the oil to see if it's bearable, and then use a muslin cloth to slowly introduce the oil into your ears.

You can also safely introduce warm olive oil, clove oil or the juice of holy basil into your ears safely.

To reduce inflammation and swelling around the ears, take the juice of garlic and ginger, pound it in a mortar and pestle or if you don't have one, grind it in a mixer, place it in a poultice bag and use it to massage around the ears—not inside the ears. Make sure there's someone else around to supervise the process and speak to an Ayurvedic doctor before administering any herbal medicines.

Skin: The first line of treatment

When I was an infant, my skin developed large open wounds that would spread over my body when it came into contact with water. My mother kept insisting that there was something wrong with the baby products she was using. She began to bathe me using only ingredients from the kitchen, such as gram flour, curd and turmeric, and my skin started to heal. Decades later, it was proven by researchers that this particular brand of baby products indeed had carcinogenic ingredients.

Even the skin and hair products we use regularly can be dangerous. A recent study by the National Cancer Institute[*] has actually linked hair-straightening chemicals to uterine cancer incidences in women.[†] Many of these products are loaded with

---

[*] American Cancer Society Medical Content, News Staff, 'Study Finds Possible Link Between Hair Straightening Chemicals and Uterine Cancer', American Cancer Society, October 26, 2022, https://www.cancer.org/cancer/latest-news/study-finds-possible-link-between-hair-straightening-chemicals-and-uterine-cancer.html, accessed on June 8, 2023.
[†] Che-Jung Chang, Katie M. O'Brien, Alexander P. Keil, Symielle A. Gaston, Chandra L. Jackson, Dale P. Sandler, Alexandra J. White, 'Use

artificial chemicals and endocrine disruptors that get absorbed into the body. Unlike food, which gets purified by the liver before entering the bloodstream, skincare products get absorbed directly through the pores in our skin. When I shared this with one of my clients who is a well-known actor and had been subjected to several harsh hair treatments, she was taken aback and remembered that, right after one such treatment, she had developed a fungal infection on her calf muscle, which soon spread all over her leg, revealing the flesh underneath. It took several months for her to reverse it.

The skin is the largest breathing organ in the human body. At any point in time, a healthy adult has 3.6 kg of skin on them, which is constantly breathing and absorbing everything you apply to it because it's a porous organ. It releases toxins through the pores in the form of sweat and absorbs creams and skincare ointments that is locally applied to treat burns and skin diseases. That is why the skin is considered the first line of treatment in Ayurveda.

Many skincare products available in the market strip our skin and hair of natural oils, and then we have to replace them with artificial moisturizers and conditioners. Follow the 80:20 rule where you use ingredients from the kitchen to wash your hair and body 80 per cent of the time. You can wash your hair with buttermilk, which is a very popular practice in India, or with rice water, which women in China have used for thousands of years. For a hair mask: soak one teaspoon of fenugreek seeds overnight; the next morning, blend it with yoghurt and then apply to your scalp and leave it on for 20–30 minutes before rinsing with cold water. To strengthen the roots, there are natural alternatives

of Straighteners and Other Hair Products and Incident Uterine Cancer', *Journal of the National Cancer Institute* DOI: https://doi.org/10.1093/jnci/djac165 (2022).

such as hibiscus powder and shikakai (Acacia concinna), which can be used as a shampoo, and moringa hair oil and coconut oil for deep conditioning. You could use plant-based yoghurt with strawberries as a hair mask for extra shine; yoghurt with banana for extra volume; yoghurt with lemon to treat dandruff; yoghurt with lemon, honey and olive oil to naturally straighten your hair; and apple cider vinegar diluted in ten parts of water as a final rinse to keep your scalp squeaky clean.

For the remaining 20 per cent of the time, for ease of use when travelling, you can use the mildest organic products available in the market. The thumb rule for skincare products is:

Apply it to your skin if you can eat it.

Chronic lifestyle diseases

I started analysing the root cause of my father's and his brother's ailments. It was poor dietary habits that had caused the accumulation of belly fat, which is directly linked to heart disorders. For my uncles, it was also a lack of exercise and suppressed emotions that caused their extreme ill health.

A few years later, my father also developed gall bladder and kidney stones, which were residual side-effects of the heavy heart medications he was on. The doctors recommended surgery. I was hell-bent against it and had a heated argument about it with my brother. My father had multiple stones of 10 mm each. I asked him to take an Ayurvedic concoction with hibiscus powder dissolved in water every night. After a few months, they were only two stones of 6.7 mm and 3.5 mm each, and the doctor himself cancelled the surgery.

The doctor was unaware of the home protocol and initially said, 'Oh you have stones because you are from Rajasthan, where the water is hard.' Funnily enough, my father left Rajasthan when he was four years old! And when the stones disappeared, the doctor said, 'Oh, sometimes the body does this on its own!' We did not bother to correct him.

When my father came out of his open-heart surgery, he contracted hepatitis B from the blood transfusion. During my divorce proceedings, his liver started to swell and the doctors advised him to go for a liver transplant. The liver is the seat of the metabolic fire, also called pitta in Ayurveda, and this is where emotions like anger, which is a hot emotion, are stored. He was severely affected by all the mental stress and emotional trauma for several weeks, just as I had feared. But the day before his scheduled liver transplant, he snapped out of his depressed state and said he was going to fix this. And he did! To this day, he wakes up and walks 9–10 km on the beach, plays tennis, swims, goes to the gym and stays very active and healthy.

I am not against modern medicine. Modern medicine is a complementary medical system, that plays a crucial role in addressing acute conditions such as fractures, heart attacks and injuries from accidents. But for all other chronic and lifestyle diseases, modern medicine only has a symptomatic-based approach, where the symptoms are suppressed and the root cause of the disease is not addressed, which is your incorrect diet and lifestyle habits. Remember, you are the author of your health and disease. Natural sciences like Ayurveda, Naturopathy, Homeopathy, yoga, and others address the root cause, the imbalances in the diet and lifestyle, and have a holistic approach to health.

What we truly need in this day and age is a level playing field for modern science and natural sciences to coexist. When these two worlds come together, we could save humanity!

Unfortunately, during colonial rule in India, many efforts were made to suppress Ayurvedic science and its teachings. The

English Education Act, passed in 1835, had funding set aside exclusively for the promotion of English language and Western science to the people. English was considered worth teaching at the cost of native languages like Sanskrit and Arabic. Medical education in indigenous languages was abolished, which heavily damaged the ayurvedic education system. The British policy was to patronize and push Western medicine, remove indigenous medicine in India, to further support the rise of chemical industries in Europe. Due to non-cooperation and lack of funds for traditional sciences, the publication of ayurvedic books came to a standstill.[*] This created a huge gap in research and development in the area of Ayurvedic herbs, preventive healthcare practices and cures, leading to a loss of confidence in this science. Turmeric and mango ginger (curcuma amada) were staple ingredients in our homecare remedies for cold, cough, fever, insomnia and skin health. Now, big pharma markets it as curcumin tablets, but they have extracted only the molecules and not the whole plant, causing them to be unstable or even ineffective, and their advice is to add black pepper to activate it and to be able to absorb the nutrients. It is unnecessary to dissect and isolate a plant molecule, when you could have used the whole plant spice in your cooking, in its natural form, where the spice is naturally in a balanced state, activated and ready for absorption and assimilation by the human body, instead of popping it in pill form, made unstable with man-made interventions and harmful preservatives?

---

[*] Sarkar, Prasanta Kumar, 'Contribution of Bengal School for the Protection of Traditional Ayurvedic Knowledge in Colonial India', *International Journal of Ayurveda Research* (2002), https://journals.lww.com/ijar/Fulltext/2022/07000/Contribution_of_Bengal_school_for_the_protection.5.aspx.

From being a primary healthcare provider, Ayurvedic science, which protected our ancestors for thousands of years, became an 'alternative' science. To this day, it is called a pseudoscience. If this is not the mafia keeping you away from 'preventive healthcare life science', then what is? Two of my Tedx speeches were blocked. In the first speech, I spoke about Ayurvedic body types and how, by eating as per your body type, you can prevent certain diseases. The speech was blocked because there were no peer reviews. During the second Tedx talk, I passionately spoke about cancer, how I avoided my fifth surgery for benign cysts using Ayurveda; how my childhood friend treated adenocarcinoma—a cancer that develops in the glands that line your organs—using only nutrition; and how one of my clients treated her cancer using only Ayurvedic *panchakarma* treatment. The speech was blocked. Sadly, preventive wellness and Ayurveda are forbidden words even in this day and age.

Several times my videos on Instagram and Facebook have been blocked when I have spoken about preventing complex diseases with an alkaline diet, which has been recorded by some scientists—who have now been silenced.* Dr Otto Warburg, a German scientist, showed through his experiments that a repeatedly oxygen-poor acidic environment can damage the tissues and cause cell mutations, leading towards cancer. The Warburg effect speaks about how acidic metabolic waste from an unhealthy diet gets released into the intestinal fluids and blood, affecting the pH level of the body (even temporarily), which can trigger complex diseases. Although this acid-base theory has been debated for many years, the truth is that we are born alkaline and we die acidic. An exploratory study conducted by Ted Greiner

---

* Hassan Bahrami, 'The Alkaline Diet and the Warburg Effect', *World Nutrition Journal*, 2021, https://worldnutritionjournal.org/index.php/wn/article/view/782/650, accessed on June 12, 2023.

and Hassan Bahrami, showed that when the scientist consumed acid-forming foods it indeed caused a drop in the pH level to 7.30, and a significant reduction in oxygen saturation in the blood. Meanwhile, alkaline forming foods allowed high oxygen saturation in the blood and the pH level rose to 7.42, which can reduce the incidence of non-communicable diseases. The study showed and I quote, 'Oxygen saturation of venous blood dropped by 33% with an acidic unhealthy diet, and oxygen saturation improved by 42% with an alkaline healthy diet. This was possibly due to diet-related metabolic wastes from the cells excreted into the veins. Also, the oxygen saturation of arterial blood increased by 94-98% when the scientists moved from an acidic diet to an alkaline diet.' This experiment further supports the need to focus on our diet to prevent chronic diseases like cancer.

During the pandemic, I conducted classes all day, teaching students how to boost their immunity in such a way that the virus could pass through the body with minimal or no collateral damage. I tested positive for Covid-19; I had a migraine for a day and zero symptoms after. I followed an Ayurvedic diet to boost my vitamins B12, C and D, and I also followed detoxification rituals to clear any unhealthy bacteria and viruses in the bronchial region. Several of our students and patients who didn't have access to allopathy medicines or hospitals due to a shortage of beds recovered at home using Ayurvedic medicines, self-detox and diet protocols. When I shared a video on this, it was blocked again by Instagram. It is a known fact that pharma companies have a vested interest even in 'fact-checkers' hired by Instagram and Facebook. And any truth that threatens their profits would be banned or blocked. The truth scares them.

Modern science is powerful when it comes to research, as long as the research material itself is not funded by pharma or FMCG companies. Because:

Food companies profit from your addiction to their foods.
Pharma profits from your disease, not your health.

Sadly, the truth is that big pharma doesn't want you to know that you can prevent diseases instead of waiting for a cure. And that the secret lies in your home, your kitchen, your diet and your lifestyle. And that you can also reverse diseases with the right nutrition. And that you need to:

Make food your medicine, not medicine your food.

If you eat the right foods, you won't need medicine. But if your dietary intake is incorrect and not personalized to your body type, even medicines won't work because the symptoms will reappear due to your consumption of contradictory foods that feed the disease.

Even worse are the packaged and heavily processed foods lining the shelves of supermarkets. There is hardly any nutrition left in them. They have unrealistic shelf lives with their harmful preservatives, so they can be sold around the world and stacked up for months together. Remember:

If food can survive on the shelf for six months,
it can survive in your gut for six months as well!

On the other hand, lentils, pulses, grains and rice have a natural shelf life that allows them to survive for up to a year without the need for artificial preservatives. They just need to be soaked overnight to get rid of those natural phytic acids that give them their shelf life, and they must be cooked really well to avoid bloating.

Learnings from my disease

My experience with cysts and surgeries also taught me the importance of being educated about our bodies. It is very important to empower our children with crucial biological information on what happens to the body during puberty; how to detect any unnatural changes, moles or fibroids; what a menstrual cycle is; what menopause is; why women experience mood swings and discomfort; how a baby is conceived and birthed; and the various feminine hygiene products and healthy non-intrusive contraceptives available. Education alone can prevent unwanted pregnancy, sexually transmitted diseases and even sexual violence among teens. You must offer them positive information before the outside world; porn and media fill their heads with negative information, which can mislead them into experimenting with their bodies to detrimental effects. Educate, empower, sensitize and raise good boys so they can have more fulfilling relationships and be there in a holistic manner for their wife, partner, sister, mother or women in general.

When you educate a girl, you educate a nation.
When you sensitize a boy, society heals and humanity
grows.

2

It All Begins . . . in the Womb!

The universe never makes mistakes.

When I was eight months old, my aunt gave me baby formula and left me alone for a few minutes. When she returned, she found me in a pool of blood. The neighbourhood cat had clawed my face and missed my eye by a millimetre. I was rushed to the hospital and put on life-saving drugs.

That was just the beginning of my health issues. I was born with epilepsy and would collapse without notice. I had a shockingly poor appetite, and my mother struggled for hours to feed me. My father took me to various hospitals for several expensive scans, which he couldn't afford at that point in time. Doctors would inject a special dye called intravenous contrast, into my little body for a brain scan to look for damaged blood vessels. But they found no answers in my brain cells or their medical books. When everything else failed, my parents turned to the many gods and bribed them with silver. When I turned eleven, the epilepsy attacks stopped on their own, only to be replaced with low blood pressure issues and excruciating migraines every single day of my teenage years. Being in pain became the new normal. But my parents kept me busy with art classes and trained me for competitive swimming, dance and violin lessons to ensure I lived a better-quality life than they had.

Often, when something breaks, we direct all our energy towards fixing it. But it is also important to take the time to understand the root cause of the event. When I look back, I realize my mother had a complicated pregnancy. She suffered from malnutrition and would throw up anything she ate. She married young and went through emotional and mental duress, adapting to this new life. All of this impacted her womb and my health.

The information I am about to share is critical for women and men.

You see, the uterus is a curious organ. It is a muscle, yet it is hollow. The muscle becomes tense under physical, emotional and mental duress. It relaxes when you relax. Much like the universe, it holds celestial space for new life to enter this world. But when this portal is damaged or plagued with diseases like PCOS, PCOD, gynaecological disorders, malnutrition, poor gut health, and mental and emotional stress, the souls that come through it suffer too.

Mother Nature offers an extra element of help when a new life is brought into this world. She placed superior stem cells in the cord blood, which can even reverse chronic diseases like cancer. When a pregnant mother struggles with her health, the foetus sends these stem cells to the mother to accelerate the healing process. Today, this cord blood is stored in cord blood banks and used to reverse diseases in immediate family members too. The female specie collectively has enough 'Qi', the circulating life force, to nourish humanity and heal the planet. That's why:

When a woman suffers,
both the human race and the planet suffer.

The uterus is home for the foetus for nine months. The health of the uterus, the health of the egg and sperm and the mother's diet during pregnancy are the four factors that determine the health of the child. Seventy per cent of a child's brain, personality and health develop in the womb; 20 per cent in the first two years; and the remaining 10 per cent in the next three years. In fact, all of us have a unique biological blueprint or genetic makeup that is fixed at the time of conception and doesn't change over an entire lifetime. This is called *prakriti* in Ayurveda—your unique biological blueprint that carries vital information on the kind of body structure you will have, functions, behaviour, mental and emotional traits, your response to internal and external stimuli, and even your susceptibility to certain diseases. It is like a manual for your body. In Chapter 5, we will learn how to identify our unique body type and design a diet and lifestyle based on the needs of our bodies.

Did you know that the uterus also stores memories? A female baby is born with a fixed number of eggs, from which you were born. Biologically speaking, you were part of your grandmother's womb as your mother's foetus was developing. You have within you all the memories of your grandmother, and she has within her all the memories of her grandmother and the many generations before. It is called genetic information or DNA in modern science, or memories in spiritual science. Our bodies have within them all the good and bad memories, diseases and trauma our ancestors have suffered, and we are by-products of the evolutionary process that came from it.

Also remember, most diseases have a psychosomatic origin and begin in the mind. When there is continuous conflict in the mind, we become unable to use our senses and intellect, to make healthy decisions. The mental conflict further leads to a disconnect between our body and our true spirit (nature), and it gets manifested into physical conflict, dis-comfort or dis-ease in our body, which simply means not at ease. When we hold negative emotions, unresolved childhood trauma, grudges, worry and pain, it gets stored in different parts of the body like the hips and uterus and translates into physical symptoms or diseases. Modern scientists have also made significant studies on how negative emotions affect the hormonal health, and immune system, changes the brain chemicals, the body's ability to fight diseases and how impacts a person's life span.[*][†][‡]

According to Vedic sciences, the human body has seven chakras, or energy points, along the spine that correspond to the nervous system, major organs and our overall physical and emotional health. Negative memories and emotional pain can get stored here, blocking the chakras and manifesting as diseases in the long run.

The first chakra is called the *Muladhara*, or root chakra, and is located at the base of the spine. It corresponds to our ability to trust. When we are unable to trust, the root chakra negatively stores fear, which can trigger disorders like anxiety, nightmares, colon and bladder health issues, lower back problems, issues with the feet and prostate health issues in men.

The second chakra is called the *Svadhisthana*, or sacral chakra, and is located below the naval. It corresponds to the kidney and reproductive organs and is responsible for our creativity and

---

[*] RW Levenson, 'Stress and Illness: A Role for Specific Emotions', *Psychosom Med* (2019).
[†] Karen Lawson, MD, 'How Do Thoughts and Emotions Affect Health?', Taking Charge of Your Health and Wellbeing, University of Minnesota, https://www.takingcharge.csh.umn.edu/how-do-thoughts-and-emotions-affect-health, accessed on June 8, 2023.
[‡] Jane E. Brody, 'Emotions Found to Influence Nearly Every Human Ailment', *New York Times,* May 24, 1984, Section C.

sexuality. But when these emotions are suppressed, the energy gets negatively stored as guilt in the sacral chakra. It can trigger issues of the spinal cord, slipped discs, anaemia, joint problems, hypoglycaemia, spleen disorders, kidney disorders and menstrual health issues in women.

The third chakra is called the *Manipura*, or solar plexus chakra and is located three fingers above the navel. It is one of the most important chakras and corresponds to wisdom and power. And the negative emotion stored here is shame. When this chakra is blocked, it can trigger stomach issues, eating disorders, ulcers, diabetes, pancreas, liver and colon health issues.

The fourth chakra is called the *Anahata*, or heart chakra, and is in the centre of the chest, above the thymus gland. This chakra corresponds to positive emotions like infinity, love, and healing, and the negative emotion stored here is grief. When this chakra is blocked, it can trigger disorders of the heart and lungs, low immunity, poor blood circulation, palpitations, frequent colds, coughs, cases of flu and infections.

The fifth chakra is called the *Vishuddha* chakra, or throat chakra, and is located in the pit of our throat. It is a powerful chakra for expression. When you are unable to express yourself clearly, exercise your choice or follow your dreams, when you lack trust and faith in life that everything will work out, or when you lie, it weakens your throat chakra. This can lead to overproduction or underproduction of the thyroid hormone, which in turn impacts your metabolic rate, nervous system, immunity, and bone and brain development. It also affects the neck, shoulder, throat and jaws, and can create feelings of depression, anxiety or low self-esteem.

The sixth chakra is called the *Ajna*, or third eye chakra, and is located in the centre of our forehead in between the eyebrows. It corresponds to positive emotions like awareness, intellectual capabilities and harmony. The negative emotion stored here is one of illusion. When this chakra gets blocked, we lose our connection with our inner wisdom and it can trigger hallucinations, disassociated feelings or feelings of being lost and stuck in life.

The seventh chakra is called the *Sahasrara*, or crown chakra, and is located on the crown of the head. It corresponds to spirituality, memory power, intelligence and our ability to focus. The negative emotion stored here is attachment. When this chakra gets blocked, it can trigger disorders of the mind like psychosis, disillusionment, boredom, melancholy, restlessness and even resistance to new ideas, thoughts and knowledge.

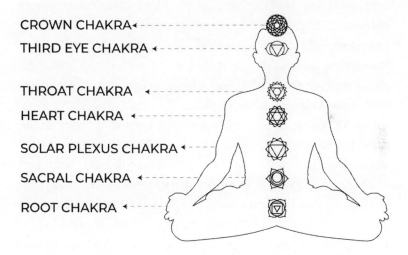

CROWN CHAKRA
THIRD EYE CHAKRA

THROAT CHAKRA
HEART CHAKRA

SOLAR PLEXUS CHAKRA

SACRAL CHAKRA

ROOT CHAKRA

Dear people, it is time to let go of all the negative memories and emotions that no longer serve you and to forgive all those who have hurt you, including lovers who didn't live up to your expectations and family and society, who failed to protect you. Forgive them and let it go. Because when you forgive, you are releasing negative memories and energy from your body. You start healing yourself, and you are healing the generations that come after you, as well as the many generations that came before you.

Exercise control over what you consume through your five senses. You will become the sum of all the books you read, the content you consume on social media, the friends you keep and the conversations you have. It is easier to filter what you consume than to struggle with emptying the junk later. Pay attention to the food on your plate because you become what you eat.

Dear women, also stay away from practices that weaken the uterus. The worst is the overuse of birth control pills prescribed without adequate reason. When someone complains of skin issues, PCOS, PCOD, endometriosis, infertility, hormonal issues or an irregular period cycle, they are prescribed birth control pills without even addressing the root cause of the disease. Moreover, they are medicated without changing their diets or lifestyles. There are external instructions given to the body using artificial stimulants and drugs with long-term side effects. And when a woman gets off long-term birth control usage, absolute chaos hits the uterus, which is suddenly put in charge again. Even women going through menopause are often put on hormonal pills to increase oestrogen, which actually contradicts the natural cycle. The body has decided not to produce oestrogen, as it is done with the birthing phase of its life.

The second-biggest harm to the uterus comes from hormones found in dairy products, meat-based foods and soya-based products. Animals get complex diseases such as cancer, hypertension, diabetes, mania and clinical depression, and are injected with harmful steroids and hormones. When you consume meat, where do the diseases and hormones go? They go into your body. Your body, white blood cells and immunity soldiers now have to work harder to destroy these animal-based hormones and potential cancer-causing cells. When you go against nature and the natural rhythm of your body, you attract disease.

When you consume animal-based foods, you also consume
the diseases the animal had.

Dairy is one of the biggest causes of gynaecological disorders
and lactose intolerance. Science says that we are lacking an
enzyme called lactase, which helps break down the sugar lactose
found in dairy products. But when you think about how our
ancestors were able to digest dairy products, gluten, and
complex foods and yet live up to 100, it makes us wonder—
what changed?

Think about it. Back in the day, milk was sourced from
farmers who treated cows like family members. Many families
had a cow of their own. The cow would feed her calf happily and
give the excess milk to the human family. Even during the worst
drought conditions, the cow would keep the family nourished
with milk, butter, cheese and cow dung, which could be used for
medicinal purposes, flooring, to ward off insects and as cooking
fuel. Children would play with the calf, which boosted their
bronchial health and overall immunity and introduced them
to healthy bacteria that aid in the digestion of lactose. There is
also an exchange of pheromonal information between the farmer
and the cow when she is bathed and fed fodder. That milk was
nourishing to our bodies—manna from heaven.

Fast forward to today. Cows are placed in factories; they are
confined and tortured, injected with steroids and hormones,
artificially inseminated and forced to give birth every year—causing
ruptured uteruses. They have machines attached to their udders
and are separated from their calves. The physical and emotional
duress makes the cows release pus, blood, cortisol and hormones
into their milk. This is the leading cause of disorders like PCOS,
PCOD, infertility, gynaecological disorders, lactose intolerance
and even cancer among humans. Be kind to yourself, and:

Don't consume cruelty.

We are the only species that drinks the milk of another animal. In fact, considering the limited availability of cruelty-free healthy milk, it is best reserved for infants whose mothers cannot produce milk, pregnant women who need extra calcium for the growth of the foetus, and senior citizens whose bones and muscles are getting emaciated. Besides them, human adults don't need milk. There is a popular saying in Asia: 'Drink the milk only if you know the cow has been treated well.'

Man-made foods such as soya milk, tofu, plant-based meat and soya chunks do not help a woman's body either. Soya has the potential to be an endocrine disruptor. It has high levels of isoflavones, which mimic oestrogen in the body and can lead to hormone overload, affect fertility, impair thyroid functions, and even promote the growth of some cancer cells. Soya isolate proteins have been made with a kind of chemical reaction, which means the vitamins and minerals get stripped away and the chemical is introduced into your body.

I ended up in the hospital for acute inflammation of my sinuses after consuming excess soya milk in my diet. Soya is considered one of the heaviest foods to digest in Ayurveda. It is a hard-to-digest protein that can impair your digestive system and is energetically considered to be a very heavy and dulling food, which can increase heaviness, mucus, the formation of fibroids, trigger thyroid issues (kapha imbalances) and also aggravate dryness and constipation (vata imbalances). Several Asians and vegans consume this as a staple diet, and their bodies become habituated to the point that they don't communicate the symptoms anymore. But the internal damage continues.

When we break the natural rhythm of the body,
we interfere with health and create room for disease.

Nourishing the uterus

The uterus responds to the cycle of the moon. It releases blood every twenty-eight days, which has a direct impact on the haemoglobin level, skin, hair, moods and emotional health. The first step is to remove the trigger foods from your diet and replace them with foods that nourish it. Incorporate iron-rich foods into your diet that help rebuild red blood cells. Foods that are green—spinach, celery, cilantro, curry leaves, moringa, spirulina, string beans, peas, asparagus, green gourd, bitter gourd, fresh fenugreek leaves and carrom leaves—are excellent sources of iron. One must also include foods that are red, such as carrots, beetroots, turnips, pomegranates and black grapes, which help generate new cells and heal the body and uterus faster. Bitter herbs like fenugreek and carrom seeds further help purify the blood, and seeds like cumin and fennel help prevent frequent urinary tract infections (UTIs).

Seed cycling is another powerful remedy—it helps heal the uterus of hormonal imbalances and diseases. During the follicular phase, starting from the last day of your period to your ovulation, you can consume two teaspoons of pumpkin and flax seeds to boost oestrogen in the body. For the next fifteen days of the luteal phase, starting from ovulation to period day, you can consume two teaspoons of sunflower and sesame seeds to boost progesterone in your body. However, avoid seed cycling if you have excess oestrogen in your body in the form of fibroids. Make sure to pre-soak all of these seeds for at least an hour or even overnight if you have weak digestion and add them to your salads or cooked foods so you can chew them well. This helps aid absorption and assimilation of these nutrients and to prevent bloating and indigestion issues. Do not add seeds to your fruits, as fruits don't require much effort to chew or digest and can cause undigested seeds to be pushed to the gut faster.

You can also include potent Ayurvedic herbs such as shatavari (asparagus racemosus), guduchi (tinospora cordifolia willd) and ashwagandha (Indian ginseng), which have adaptogenic, anti-inflammatory and antioxidant properties that help heal the uterus. Speak to an Ayurvedic doctor before consuming any herb, as herbs are potent and should not be consumed unless there are symptoms.

If you are planning to conceive, you can even get a full body cleanse done through an Ayurvedic panchakarma treatment, which helps flush out all the toxins, especially from the digestive system, colon and uterus. This way, you can ensure a safe home for your baby for the next nine months.

During pregnancy, new mothers can incorporate sweet herbs such as shatavari (asparagus racemosus), yastimadhu (liquorice), gulkand (rose petal jam), brahmi (maska pennywort) and vidari (maska kudzu) to improve lactation and foetal health.

Should you work out during your menstrual cycle?

Let us first understand what happens in a woman's body during the menstrual cycle. According to Ayurveda, vata, or a downward-moving wind principle, gets activated near the uterus, which allows the uterus to shed its lining in the form of blood. It is not advisable to do any counterproductive upward movements, such as inserting tampons or menstrual cups, engaging in sexual intercourse, doing aggressive physical exercises or even inversion asanas. Do minimal workouts if you really need to.

You should load up on foods that are rich in iron—leafy greens, spinach, celery, cilantro, curry leaves, moringa, spirulina, French beans and peas—which help rebuild red blood cells in the body. You could also consume carrots, beetroots, pomegranates and black grapes during this time. Stay away from dairy products during your period because they confuse the body. The excess oestrogen is difficult to digest and it can actually trigger vaginal discharge. In Ayurveda, dairy products like curd and buttermilk are actually forbidden during periods. Take a lot of rest and give in to your cravings, even if they're in the form of chocolate and ice cream—choose vegan options and consume in moderation.

Childbirth

Here is another bit of critical information that will shape your perception of childbirth. When a child has a natural vaginal birth, they are covered in vaginal fluid, which contains the vaginal flora or bacteria. Babies born vaginally use these microbes to build their gut health, which helps them build immunity and fight diseases. In complex situations where a C-section is unavoidable and necessary to save a child's and mother's lives, modern medicine comes to the rescue. But when you have a choice, choose a vaginal birth for the sake of your child's health and your own. Epidurals and the cocktail of painkillers introduced at the time of childbirth, unfortunately, expose the newborn to their effects too. Vaginal birth for the infant is a process that could be compared to a butterfly emerging from the cocoon on its own. When the butterfly naturally struggles its way out of the cocoon, it forces blood into its wings, which gives it strength and firmness, and thus, the ability to fly.

Prepare yourself mentally and ask your gynaecologist for a normal delivery from the start. Enrol for foetal education, which is also called 'garbha sanskar' in Ayurveda. It offers all the necessary tools for a dietary protocol for different months of pregnancy, dos and don'ts for the new mother, recipes, remedies and detoxification rituals to prevent post-partum health issues. You can also choose water birthing in a serene and calm environment with the help of a midwife or birthing therapist. Remember, the first sounds, sights, smells and words will be forever imprinted in your child's subconscious mind. Let that atmosphere not be one of fear and trauma instead of a welcoming environment filled with love.

Post-partum, the mother's body heals faster when it is a natural delivery. The first exercise you must do is *pranayam*—relearning how to breathe to adjust the diaphragm below the lungs, which may have been pushed during pregnancy. There are fasting rituals and detoxification rituals in Ayurveda to remove any placenta, baby poop, or bad bacteria that is left inside, and there are special recipes to improve lactation. Fumigation of the vagina is done to heal the uterus, while *abhyangam* (full body oil massage) brings the bones and muscles back into place and facilitates early recovery. Meanwhile, the umbilical cord is sundried for several days by the eldest woman in the family, converted into powder form, placed inside a silver locket and tied around the child's waist. For the first five years, whenever the infant has a serious illness, the mother unlocks the locket, takes a pinch of this cord powder and gives it to the child. Today, this process has been commercialized by cord blood banks at exorbitant prices.

Breastfeeding builds better immunity and a bond. When a mother holds her baby close to her, she receives pheromonal information from the baby's scalp, which travels through her olfactory senses into her brain. The brain deciphers the information on the baby's nutritional deficiencies and sends a message to the breast milk factory on the formulation of milk to produce. In fact, a mother's milk varies between her two children as well as between two feeds for the same child! Twins may prefer one side of the mother's breast because they have already communicated their individual nutritional needs.

But most importantly, whether you choose to bring life into this world or not is your personal choice. Honour your body, your desires, the power of creation and the power of choice. Honour the divinity within you. You can be anything you want—a career-driven professional, a domestic Goddess, an artist, a mother, a wife, a daughter, a sister, a teacher, a guide or a free-spirited single woman existing in perfect harmony with her higher truth.

You can have it all, but the balance lies in choosing the exact roles you want to play. Because:

The most important relationship you will have
is the one with yourself.

3

Unravelling the Mysteries of the Gut

Medically speaking, the gut is where food passes through after digestion and it includes the small intestine and the large intestine, where the absorption and assimilation of nutrients happen, and the colon, where the elimination of waste takes place. Some scientists believe that the gut also includes organs such as the mouth, which is home to trillions of oral bacteria; the oesophagus; the stomach and all the organs that support the digestion process—the liver, gall bladder and pancreas. These provide bile and digestive enzymes to further aid the digestion process.

Did you know that:

> *An unhealthy colon is the root cause of 90 per cent of diseases.*

Barely 10 per cent of diseases are caused by external factors like dengue, malaria and epidemics. Most are caused due to internal factors, such as poor diet, lifestyle and unhealthy habits. This was recently proven by several researchers[*][†][‡] that poor gut health and microbiome can impact neural health, and emotional behaviour, and can cause diseases right from constipation to the common cold, cancer, and clinical depression. But it was emphasized in Ayurvedic texts 5000 years ago that maintaining digestive health, a healthy metabolic fire and the elimination of toxins were critical to good health.

The colon is also one of the most neglected organs in the human body. There is so little education around it and, quite often, people are embarrassed to discuss their colon health issues with their family members.

Constipation is the beginning of all trouble. Take the trash out! Every single day! What happens when you don't take the trash out of your kitchen? The whole house starts to smell of decomposed waste, which attracts flies and insects. If you don't eliminate waste on a daily basis, it can rupture the colon lining, get leaked or re-absorbed into the bloodstream and circulate back to your other vital organs, like the brain, heart, liver, kidney and skin. Also, the same blood that is circulating in your colon also circulates in your brain. This is why, when we are constipated, we feel irritable, snappy, moody and like 'crap'. People say, 'Oh, he is

---

[*] Dr Siri Carpenter, 'That Gut Feeling', *American Psychological Association* Vol 43, No. 8 (2012), https://www.apa.org/monitor/2012/09/gut-feeling, accessed June 8, 2023.

[†] Alistair Gardine, 'Poor Gut Health Can Lead to These Chronic Diseases', MDLinx, July 15, 2021, https://www.mdlinx.com/article/poor-gut-health-can-lead-to-these-chronic-diseases/1TzMRXobWPsfZfqAKgoVMM, accessed June 8, 2023.

[‡] YJ Zhang, S. Li, RY Gan, T. Zhou, D.P. Xu, H.B. Li, 'Impacts of Gut Bacteria on Human Health and Diseases', *International Journal of Molecular Science* (2015), https://www.ncbi.nlm.nih.gov/pmc/articles/PMC4425030/, June 8, 2023.

90% OF DISEASES ARE TRIGGERED DUE TO AN UNHEALTHY COLON

PSYCHOSOMATIC	ANXIETY, STRESS, SYMPTOMS OF DEPRESSION BRAIN FOG, INABILITY TO FOCUS MIND-BODY COORDINATION ISSUES MOOD SWINGS, IRRITABILITY FATIGUE, LACK OF MOTIVATION
BRONCHIAL HEALTH	ALLERGIES, FREQUENT COLD, FLU INFLAMED SINUS, NASAL DRIPPING ASTHMA, HAY FEVER CONGESTION OF AIR PASSAGES
GASTRO INTESTINAL HEALTH	BLOATING, GAS, BURPING HYPERACIDITY, REFLUX, HEARTBURN CANCER
GUT HEALTH	ANAEMIA, MALNUTRITION MALABSORPTION SYNDROME LEAKY GUT SYNDROME ABDOMINAL DISTENTION AND PAIN
SKIN HEALTH	PSORIASIS, ECZEMA, ROSACEA PIMPLES, ACNE VARICOSE VEINS
MUSCULOSKELETAL HEALTH	ARTHRITIS MUSCLE ACHES
GYNAECOLOGICAL HEALTH	YEAST INFECTIONS, VAGINAL DISCHARGE PCOS, PCOD, INFERTILITY YEAST INFECTIONS, UTI, PMS SYMPTOMS CANCER
COLON HEALTH	CONSTIPATION, DIARRHOEA, FLATULENCE IRRITABLE BOWEL SYNDROME SPASTIC COLON, DIVERTICULITIS CROHN'S DISEASE, COLON POLYPS COLON CANCER
LOWER LIMBS	COLD EXTREMITIES ATHLETE'S FOOT, TOE NAIL FUNGUS

stuck up' or 'she is so full of it', which translates to being difficult or constipated. On the days you are constipated, your productivity and energy levels also get impacted and you will struggle to think clearly. But the day you have a clean bowel movement, you feel like you can conquer the world.

Your gut is made up of the small intestine, which is about twenty-two feet long; the large intestine, which is about six feet long; and a small colon bag. That is the height of a four-storey building! Imagine if all the drainage pipes in this four-storey building got blocked. No matter how beautiful your home is from the outside, the whole building is going to reek. The same is true for your colon. You must keep the passageway clean and well-lubricated.

Diseases usually begin with simple symptoms such as constipation, indigestion and irritable bowel syndrome, and go on to trigger serious issues including bronchial disorders, neurological disorders, psychosomatic disorders, gastrointestinal disorders, gynaecological disorders, musculoskeletal disorders, skin diseases and even cancer.

Leaky gut syndrome

Leaky gut syndrome is another major health issue preoccupying doctors today. It is the root cause of many diseases we experience in our bodies.

The epithelial cells lining the small intestine are held together by tight occluding junctions, which act as a barrier. This helps keep the gut contents and the undigested food in the gut while allowing the transformed nutrients to pass through into the bloodstream. When we consume packaged foods and junk foods, it feeds the harmful bacteria in our gut, which can damage these junctions and cause bigger gaps to form. The gut starts to leak undigested food, toxic waste and unhealthy bacteria into the bloodstream, which gets circulated to other organs. In a desperate attempt to get rid of the toxins, the body tries to push them towards the surface of the skin, hoping to get rid of them through the pores in the form of sweat. But when the toxins are too big, they get deposited under the skin, triggering psoriasis, eczema, pimples, acne and other inflammatory conditions.

Leaky gut syndrome cannot be detected through scans or X-rays. You will simply experience symptoms and discomfort. It leads to malabsorption of nutrients, food intolerances, frequent colds and headaches due to weak immunity, leakage of calcium from your bones causing bone-related disorders, hormonal disruption causing thyroid issues, Hashimoto's disease, Graves, serious skin disorders, damage to the nervous system triggering fibromyalgia (unexplained body aches and pain), and other psychosomatic imbalances such as anxiety, stress and symptoms of depression. When toxins are leaked into the blood, the body also triggers an auto-immune reaction in response to these foreign substances and starts attacking all the good and bad cells. Your body is now in a state of conflict and at war with itself.

You will often experience a drop in your adrenals, fatigue, a lack of energy no matter how well you eat and a loss of appetite. The gut starts sending distress signals continuously to the brain, which can trigger headaches. Inflammation from the presence of leaked toxins, the build-up of gases from indigestion, and inflamed sinuses are other triggers for headaches. A lack of helpful gut bacteria can also lead to an overgrowth of bad bacteria and trigger leaky gut syndrome. In this book, we will explore all the Ayurvedic tools and remedies that will help repair the gut lining, remove trigger foods and reset our gut back to good health.

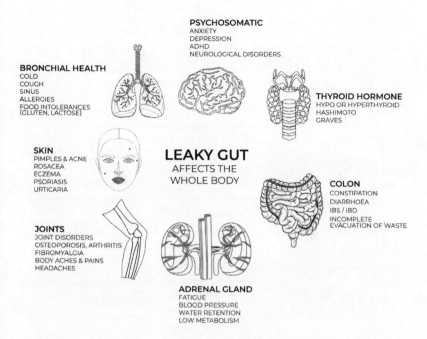

PSYCHOSOMATIC
ANXIETY
DEPRESSION
ADHD
NEUROLOGICAL DISORDERS

BRONCHIAL HEALTH
COLD
COUGH
SINUS
ALLERGIES
FOOD INTOLERANCES
(GLUTEN, LACTOSE)

THYROID HORMONE
HYPO OR HYPERTHYROID
HASHIMOTO
GRAVES

SKIN
PIMPLES & ACNE
ROSACEA
ECZEMA
PSORIASIS
URTICARIA

LEAKY GUT
AFFECTS THE
WHOLE BODY

COLON
CONSTIPATION
DIARRHOEA
IBS / IBD
INCOMPLETE
EVACUATION OF WASTE

JOINTS
JOINT DISORDERS
OSTEOPOROSIS, ARTHRITIS
FIBROMYALGIA
BODY ACHES & PAINS
HEADACHES

ADRENAL GLAND
FATIGUE
BLOOD PRESSURE
WATER RETENTION
LOW METABOLISM

Vital information coming out of your body

Your poop shows early signs of disease. New mothers often check the stools of their babies for signs of mucus, worms or discolouration in general. If there is green discolouration, it signifies excess phlegm and mucus built up in the child's body. The discoloration in your stools also tells you which part of the body is being detoxified (*see following chart*). It is both a good and a warning sign that there might be more toxins in your body, and you must support the detoxification process by going on a simple mono-diet or a fruit diet.

Mono dieting

Here is a simple tool to help with the detoxification process at home. Mono (monotrophic) dieting, means having the same

COLOR OF YOUR STOOL & THE ORGAN DETOXIFIED

COLOR OF PARTICLE	PART OF THE BODY DETOXIFYING
BLACK	TOXINS FROM LIVER, SYMPTOMS OF GASTRITIS, GASTRIC ULCERS, BLEEDING IN THE UPPER PART OF THE DIGESTIVE SYSTEM OR PRESENCE OF ACTIVATED CHARCOAL
BLACK FLECKS	HEAVY METALS, PRESERVATIVES FROM PACKAGED FOODS
BROWN	TOXINS FROM THE LIVER, CELLULAR WASTE, AIR POLLUTANTS
DARK GREEN	TOXINS FROM THE GALLBLADDER, EXCESSIVE IRON SUPPLEMENTS OR LICORICE IN DIET
ORANGE	TOXINS FROM THE JOINTS, OR SYMPTOMS OF IBS, CYSTS, GALLSTONES
RED FLECKS	EXCESSIVE BEETROOT AND TOMATO IN DIET, BLOOD CLOTS FROM TISSUES, HAEMORRHOIDS, ANAL FISSURES, DIVERTICULITIS, ULCERATIVE COLITIS, BLEEDING IN THE LOWER INTESTINES, OR COLON CANCER
WHITE PARTICLES	YEAST INFECTION, FUNGAL INFECTION, OR LACK OF BILE
FROTHY, GREASY	DEFICIENCY OF VITAMIN A, D, E, K2
WHITE FOAM	TOXINS FROM THE LYMPHATIC SYSTEM, GIARDIA PARASITE, BACTERIAL INFECTION
YELLOW GREEN	KIDNEY, BLADDER, URINARY TRACT, REPRODUCTIVE ORGANS, CELIAC, GIARDIA OR GUT INFECTION
MUCUS IN STOOLS	ULCERATIVE COLITIS, CROHN'S DISEASE, IRRITABLE BOWEL SYNDROME

meal every day for a few days till your body is cleansed from the inside. It gives much-needed rest to your digestive system. Your pancreas, gall bladder, liver, stomach and intestines have to digest the same meal every day, which gives them adequate free energy to detoxify. The liver is the largest detoxifying organ in our bodies, but due to the many complex foods we consume, it is preoccupied with only digesting them. In fact, there is a joke that the liver has the memory of a goldfish and looks at every meal as if it's seeing it for the first time. Mono-dieting gives the liver a much-needed break from having to calculate how to digest complex food groups.

Now don't go to extremes and try a mono diet with chocolate, dairy or just bananas, as it could lead to nutritional deficiencies, imbalances and loss of muscle. Khichdi, comprising rice, mung beans, turmeric, basic vegetables, condiments and warm spices, is the perfect meal for mono dieting, striking a perfect balance between carbohydrates, proteins and fibre. Consume this for lunch and dinner for three, four, five or eight days, and watch how your body transforms.

When you return to a normal diet, make sure to include at least one bowl of fruits, one bowl of steamed vegetables and a bowl of warm soup in your diet every day to strengthen your gut flora. Sip warm herbal teas made with spices such as cumin, fennel, coriander, carrom and cardamom to improve digestive juices.

In fact, when the weather changes, Ayurveda recommends mono dieting to give your digestive system a well-deserved break, and adequate time to acclimatize to the new season. During the spring equinox, the sun shines directly on the equator, marking the end of winter and the birth of spring. Engage in spring cleaning of not just your physical spaces but also your mental, emotional, spiritual and energetic spaces. Let go of memories that don't serve you anymore, because any memory that stays in your body for longer than it should is going to cause havoc. Let go of impurities and toxins in your body by engaging in a juice cleanse, mono dieting and the Ayurvedic panchakarma treatment. And celebrate what nature offers us in abundance: fresh food, clean air and sunshine.

4

'I Have a Gut Feeling'

'I have a heart feeling' or 'a brain feeling', said no one ever. It is a gut feeling, gut intuition, or gut instinct that we all crave to experience and follow. Have you ever had a gut feeling about something, and when you followed what it was telling you, it was the best decision you made? But how is it possible for us to feel through the gut? Shouldn't our feelings come from a purer place, like the heart centre, or a more superior organ, like the brain?

We always follow our gut because, deep down, even our bodies know that:

Intuition comes from the gut!

Many scientists call the gut 'a second brain' or the enteric nervous system (ENS). One could even say that the gut is the biggest brain in the body because there are more neurons (100 million nerve cells) lining the gut walls than there are neurons in the brain. Neurons are your information messengers that transmit information between different areas within the brain and also between the brain and the nervous system, which is connected to all the other organs.[*]

The gut is directly connected to the brain

The gut has a hotline to the brain. It sends messages to the brain every microsecond. The vagus nerve, or vagal nerve, plays a critical role here, controlling the gut–brain axis and carrying messages from the digestive system and organs to the brain and vice versa. It originates from the brainstem, passes through the neck and the thorax, down to the abdomen, and controls bodily functions such as digestion, heart rate and the immune system. In fact, scientists have discovered[†] [‡] that treating the vagus nerve allows us to address psychiatric disorders such as depression and PTSD, as well as gastrointestinal disorders such as indigestion and irritable bowel syndrome.

---

[*] Debra Bradley Ruder, 'The Enteric Nervous System That Regulates Our Gut Is Often Called the Body's "Second Brain"', Harvard Medical School, 2017, https://hms.harvard.edu/news-events/publications-archive/brain/gut-brain#:~:text=The%20enteric%20nervous%20system%20that,brain%20when%20something%20is%20amiss, accessed June 8, 2023.

[†] S. Breit, A. Kupferberg, G. Rogler, G. Hasler, 'Vagus Nerve as Modulator of the Brain-Gut Axis in Psychiatric and Inflammatory Disorders', *Front Psychiatry* (2018), https://www.ncbi.nlm.nih.gov/pmc/articles/PMC5859128/, accessed on June 8, 2023.

[‡] Scott T. Aaronson, M.D., Peter Sears, C.C.R.P., et al, 'A 5-Year Observational Study of Patients with Treatment-Resistant Depression Treated With Vagus Nerve Stimulation or Treatment as Usual: Comparison of Response, Remission, and Suicidality', *The American Journal of Psychology* (2017), https://ajp.psychiatryonline.org/doi/10.1176/appi.ajp.2017.16010034, accessed on June 8, 2023.

Sing, hum and chant your way to good gut health!

The vagus nerve is the most sensitive and also the weakest nerve. It governs the respiratory system, digestive system and neuron health and sends messages to the gut on when to churn the food, what kind of enzyme production to keep, how much stomach acid to maintain and when to contract which muscle in order to push the food into the intestines. When these signals are strong or at a high vagal tone, it signifies healthy digestion and your ability to adapt to stress. But when these signals are weak, it signifies a low vagal tone and poor digestive health.

How can we strengthen the vagal nerve at home? The vagus nerve is also directly connected to your vocal cord and the muscles at the back of your throat. You can sing, hum, chant, gargle with a mixture of warm water, turmeric and salt, and do the *brahmi pranayama* to strengthen the vagus nerve. You see, the morning prayers and songs our mothers made us sing were not just meant to please God but to improve our gut health too.

Chanting not only strengthens the vagal nerve and digestion, but it also improves mental health by replacing any negative sounds in our brain with positive ones. It improves focus, mental clarity, concentration and coordination.

The gut and brain have a 1:1 relationship.

It is almost like a marriage between two equals and, for a healthy relationship, both must have equal opportunities to express themselves. While you are busy relishing a piece of dessert, your brain sends messages to the gut about what kind of food is about to arrive and what kind of digestive juices to prepare for the new guest. Meanwhile, your gut continuously sends feedback to the brain on how it is feeling, when it is full and when to stop eating. However, when we sit with poor posture, the gut–brain axis gets impacted, causing delayed signals from the gut to the brain, leading to overeating. This is why, in many Asian cultures, elders emphasize the importance of sitting on the floor to eat. When you sit cross-legged, it corrects the posture of your spine and allows your gut and brain to smoothly communicate, which prevents you from overeating.

Emotions are experienced in the gut

When you feel anxious, scared, excited, happy or nervous, where do you feel it? You first feel it in the gut. You experience butterflies fluttering in the stomach, and if you entered a place that holds a negative vibe, you would also have this gut-wrenching feeling that something is not right. And your gut is never wrong. It is like a compass installed inside you to help you navigate smoothly through this world. Listen to it.

Memories are also stored in the gut.

When we eat a delicacy that is similar to our grandmother's recipe, nostalgia hits. Suddenly, our minds get flooded with all our childhood memories! In fact, advertisers will use that emotion to sell you packaged food products. That is because emotions are experienced through touch, taste, sound and smell, and the sum of those emotions is stored in the form of memories. Your gut responds to those memories by reminding you exactly how you felt before. The neurons in your brain and your gut make memories by firing together, which allows you to recall multiple memories at the same time. So, emotions and memories are also stored in the gut, and you have an added reason to protect it.

Over 75 per cent of serotonin is released in the gut

Serotonin is the 'feel-good hormone' that plays a key role in fighting anxiety and depression. When the gut is healthy and happy, it sends positive signals to the brain. But when the gut is unhealthy, it sends distress signals to the brain. When we eat a simple home-cooked meal that is made with fresh ingredients and lovingly prepared by our grandparents, parents, partners or even ourselves, we naturally feel satiated and happy due to the serotonin released in the gut. But when we eat reheated, packaged foods that have preservatives and a short shelf life, the feeling isn't the same. The gut responds to the quality of the ingredients and the cooking methods and releases serotonin accordingly.

The way to everybody's heart is through the gut!

But God forbid, if you were experiencing indigestion, bloating, flatulence, hyperacidity, reflux or irritable bowel syndrome, would you be able to enjoy a romantic dinner date or even pay attention to your partner? No. Because your gut supersedes your brain and bombards it with so many messages, you would not be able to focus.

Similarly, comfort foods also help during times of distress by releasing serotonin in the gut, which helps reduce anxiety. This is why a tub of ice-cream works as comfort food during a heartbreak or an emotional meltdown. It numbs the pain by releasing serotonin. But remember, this is an indulgence for occasional moments. After giving yourself a decent break, remember to dust yourself off and get back on the horse. Don't let this event and junk eating cascade out of control.

Your GI tract is sensitive to emotions

The GI (gastrointestinal) tract, or the gut–brain axis, is also sensitive to emotions. If you are feeling stressed, your digestion gets impaired, and that subsequently impacts your ability to focus. When you eat in an angry mood, it can trigger excess heat in the digestive system and cause acidity, reflux and a burning sensation. This is called an imbalance in the fire element (pitta) in Ayurveda. It proves that your body and mind have a powerful 1:1 relationship.

Quite often, we end up using food to suppress our emotions. Overeating creates a feeling of fullness, which mirrors the chaos and heaviness in the mind. Overthinking causes the digestive process to get stressed, as the brain is unable to focus on the signals from the digestive system. Eating too fast can also impair the communication signals between the gut and the brain.

Next time you feel negative, sit down and drink a glass of water. Come to a state of calm before you address the food on your plate. In many religions and cultures around the world, people say a little prayer and express gratitude before having a meal. This simply pauses the overthinking in the brain, and gratitude activates the parasympathetic nervous system, which improves digestion. Remember this:

You have on your plate what many people around the world don't.

The most powerful thing in the world is . . . one grain of rice

It is said that when a grain of rice is offered with devotion, you can even satiate the hunger of the gods. Why is it so powerful? Let's look at its journey. The farmer has toiled for hours, putting in his sweat and blood to grow this harvest. He slept hungry on some days to make sure there was food on your plate. The sun has selflessly shone, water and air have nourished the plant, and the plant—after growing to its fullest growth potential—has given its body to nourish yours.

What can you do to honour this food and your body?

Proper posture. Sit on the ground in *sukhasana*, which is also called the easy pose, with your legs crossed. When you rest the lower part of your body, your body has more blood available for circulation to the digestive system. The grounding from Mother Nature also calms the nervous system. This posture also puts less stress on the gut–brain axis, which can now smoothly communicate and send the right signals. Ensure there are no distractions—mobile phones or laptops—when you're eating, so your brain can focus on the signals from the digestive system. Your gut and brain work together to digest the food that you eat.

Donate food. If you're in a restaurant and there is leftover food, just order a few more pieces of bread or roti, or some rice, make a nice meal out of it and give it to someone on the street. Remember, there are several kids who go to bed hungry but thanks to you, there could be one less hungry child. And the joy of giving is unparalleled. There is a proverb in India that goes, *'Every grain of rice belongs to the person who eats it.'*

Gut health impacts your mental and emotional health

At any point in time, a healthy gut has trillions of bacteria. Good bacteria aid in the digestion of the foods you eat. You can further improve your good bacteria with healthy probiotics in the form of fresh fruits and fermented foods. This also impacts your serotonin and dopamine levels and activates your parasympathetic nervous system, which is the calming part of the nervous system. Research shows that good gut bacteria[*] [†]can also relieve symptoms of anxiety, stress, depression and enhance your moods, whereas bad bacteria can lead to gut dysbiosis and inflammation, and has been linked to several mental health issues like anxiety and depression. Remember the equation:

Healthy food nourishes good bacteria,
unhealthy food fuels bad bacteria.

What are the unhealthy foods you must stay away from? Refined foods. Refined sugar is the most dangerous of all. It has the same impact on your brain as that of hard drugs and acts as fuel for bad bacteria. Refined oils, refined salt, packaged foods, deep-fried foods and carbonated drinks—all of these are so finely processed that they cause holes in the gut and leak into the bloodstream, causing inflammation and chronic health issues. Refined flour used in pizzas, burgers, breads and pasta is the most inedible food. It turns into a sticky glue-like substance and gets stuck to the gut lining for days and weeks together. Other food particles begin to stick to this glue-like substance, which becomes a breeding ground for bad bacteria to multiply uncontrollably, even causing fermentation and gases. When bad bacteria multiply, your mental health also gets impacted. Every time you are about to eat, ask yourself:

---

[*] Dr Siri Carpenter, 'That Gut Feeling', *American Psychological Association* Vol 43, No. 8 (2012), https://www.apa.org/monitor/2012/09/gut-feeling, accessed on June 8, 2023.

[†] M. Clapp, N. Aurora, L. Herrera, et al, Gut Microbiota's Effect on Mental Health: The Gut-Brain Axis', Clinical Practice (2017), https://www.ncbi.nlm.nih.gov/pmc/articles/PMC5641835/, accessed on June 8, 2023.

Am I feeding my good bacteria or bad bacteria . . . and thus, my mental health.

Psychosocial factors influence the physiology of the gut as well

When you are stressed, it has a direct impact on the movements and contractions of the GI tract. It is a proven medical fact that many people with functional gastrointestinal disorders perceive pain more acutely. In the coming chapters, we will learn how to negate stress and build a more positive environment around us.

An unhealthy gut impacts neurological health

If your gut is unhealthy, it can lead to malnourishment of the nervous system and cause toxins to block it. It can also lead to neurological imbalances such as lack of coordination, lack of concentration, mood swings, irritability, anxiety, depression and insomnia, as well as Parkinson's and Alzheimer's.

Your gut health impacts your skin and hair

In the event of leaky gut syndrome, your body goes into survival mode and saves essential nutrients for vital organs like the heart, liver, kidneys and brain, because it wants you to stay alive! Sadly, skin and hair are considered superficial and are the last to receive nutrition from the gut. In this event, they would receive little to no nutrition at all! And the unhealthy bacteria, undigested foods and toxins leaked from the gut get deposited under the skin, affecting the skin microbiota and triggering psoriasis, eczema, urticaria and other skin disorders.

You become what you eat

The skin is a powerful indicator and a visual representation of your internal health. Growing up, you may have heard your grandma say, 'Why is your skin unhealthy? Are you not flushing your bowels clean?' Ayurveda and Chinese medicine follow a face map, which recognizes that different parts of the face correspond to specific internal organs. The presence of toxins in any organ first manifests as pimples, acne and pigmentation in those corresponding parts of the face.

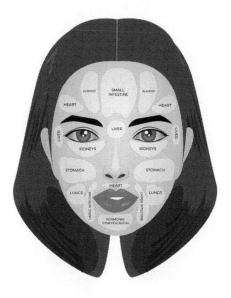

FACE MAPPING
WHAT DOES ACNE REVEAL
ABOUT YOUR HEALTH?

A diet with fresh organic foods can give you healthy, glowing skin, whereas excess alcohol and sugar in your diet can cause your skin to appear dull and lifeless. A diet comprising good fats can help the skin release more sebum, while excessive dry foods in the diet can cause the skin to dry up because these raw foods borrow from and deplete your good fats to aid digestion. A diet of astringent foods—apples, berries, cherries, strawberries and hummus—helps reduce oxidative stress in the body, tightens the collagen and reverses the ageing process.

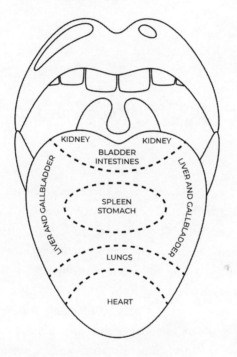

Similarly, your tongue is a visual map of your internal health. Ayurvedic doctors examine your tongue and look for discolouration or abnormalities on different parts of the tongue to gauge what is wrong. I remember this young boy having frequent blackouts. The doctor examined his tongue and said there was a blood clot in a specific part of the brain. And, during the CT scan, he was proved right! Luckily, things were at an early stage and the boy was immediately treated.

5

Your Unique Biological Blueprint

'Ayurveda' means knowledge of life or the science of life. It is based on the principles of Mother Nature and is like a manual on how to take care of this body that we have been gifted by nature. It is a personalized science that helps you design a diet and lifestyle based on your unique body composition, age, gender, genetic factors, seasonal factors, lifestyle, and family history of diseases so that you can live a long and healthy life. It is a curative and preventive healthcare life science that provides the body with the necessary nutrients to boost immunity and taps into the body's intuitive intelligence to heal. It is like a language that Mother Nature uses to communicate with our bodies through herbs and medicines, and we use this language to communicate with our food and gut.

Ayurveda states that *one size doesn't fit all*. And Ayurveda celebrates that. No two human beings and no two digestive systems are the same. Our diet must be personalized to our unique body type. Each one of us was born with a unique biological blueprint, which holds vital information about our health and susceptibility to diseases. Ayurveda plays a powerful role here in helping prevent those diseases.

Ayurveda is also called the mother of all sciences. It has eight branches that deal with the study of herbs, surgery, ENT, paediatrics, toxicology, psychiatry, geriatrics and fertility.

Here is a fun fact: did you know that surgery was invented by Ayurveda?[*] Ayurvedic physician Sushruta, who is called the father of surgery, conducted the first set of complex surgeries in 600 BCE, including cosmetic, plastic and dental surgery, and there are records of complicated surgeries such as Caesarean, cataract, fixing of artificial limbs, repairing of fractures, removal of urinary stones and even rhinoplasty. Modern science borrowed extensively from these natural sciences and developed them further with research and development and modern precision surgery tools.

Five superior elements

Your body is made up of five elements: earth, water, fire, air and space, which is called *pancha-mahabhoot* in Ayurveda. This is the basis of this earth, the oceans, land, foods, animals, birds, humans and the entire universe. When we are born, we are in the purest form of these elements, and when we die, we disintegrate back into these elements. Between life and death, the play and dominance of these elements determine the quality of our health and lives.

Earth: The food that you eat comes from the earth element and helps build your gross body and tissues.

---

[*] V. Singh, 'Sushruta: The Father of Surgery', *National Journal of Maxillofacial Surgery* (2017), https://www.ncbi.nlm.nih.gov/pmc/articles/PMC5512402/#:~:text=Ayurveda%20is%20one%20of%20the,is%20the%20father%20of%20surgery, accessed on June 8, 2023.

Water: Water makes up 75 per cent of your gross body and over 80 per cent of your brain. We consume water in various forms: cooked foods, fruits, fluids and juices.

Fire: We have a warm energy in our bodies that keeps us alive. It helps digest food, absorb and assimilate nutrients, and convert these nutrients into *saptadhatu* (the seven layers of tissues) in our bodies, like plasma, blood, muscles (which include skin), adipose (good fats and all fluids in our bodies), bones (which include teeth, nails and hair), bone marrow (which includes the nervous system), sperm and eggs.

Air: We have air in our lungs, bones, stomach, intestines, colon and all the other organs, which keeps us alive.

Ether: We experience ether or space in our mind and spaces in our bones and organs.

Three biological building blocks

The above five elements come together to make doshas, the three biological building blocks of our bodies. They are vata, pitta and kapha.

Kapha: Imagine you have been given dry clay and water. When they are mixed, this clay can be moulded into a pot. It gets a physical form. Similarly, earth and water come together to make our gross body, which is also called kapha. It provides structure, support, stability and a physical form to our bodies by building bones, muscles, tissues, teeth, nails and hair. When kapha is in a state of balance, it leads to good bone and tissue development. But when there is an excess of kapha in our bodies, it leads to the accumulation of mucus, water and fat in the body and triggers symptoms of cold, cough, sinus, allergies, asthma, hay fever, lung congestion, bronchial issues, obesity, high cholesterol and heart-related ailments.

Pitta: Imagine the wet clay pot again. You have done a fine job making it, but it is still not ready for use. The potter places your design in the kiln to bake it and transform it into a usable object. Similarly, fire and water come together to become the transformative fire in our bodies, which is called 'pitta' in Ayurveda. It is responsible for all kinds of digestive and transformative processes in our bodies. It transforms food into digestive juices, the juices into nutrients, and further transforms the nutrients into the seven layers of tissues called *saptadhatu* in Ayurveda, which are plasma, blood, adipose, muscles (and skin), bones (teeth, nails and hair), bone marrow (and the nervous system), and the reproductive system (sperm and eggs). The eighth tissue, or bonus tissue, is called *ojas* in Ayurveda, which means 'essence of life'. When all seven tissues are nourished, it helps build ojas, which nourishes our mental and emotional health, sweetens our relationships and strengthens our spiritual journey.

Now, the digestive fire in our gut is called *agni* in Ayurveda and it is responsible for the digestion, absorption and assimilation of nutrients. This agni is the source of life and literally keeps us alive. At zero degrees, we are as good as dead. If balanced, it helps build new tissues and keeps our bodies energetic and young. But when pitta (fire and water) is in excess, it triggers disorders of the stomach, small intestine, skin, sweat glands and fat, where it is dominant. It can cause inflammation in the body, discolouration of the eyes, excessive sweating, skin diseases, hyperacidity, reflux, and gastroesophageal reflux disease (GERD). The liver, gall bladder and stomach are the most sensitive to imbalances in the fire element and react with abdominal distention, indigestion and stomach-related ailments.

Vata: The pot has been taken out of the furnace or kiln, but it is still not ready for use. You have to leave the pot in the open air for it to reach its final stage. Similarly, earth and water came together to make the gross body; fire gives digestive and transformative fire to the body; and air literally breathes life into this body. Air and ether come together to form vata, which is responsible for all kinds of movements in our bodies. The movement of thoughts in our mind, the movement of food from the mouth to the stomach, intestines and colon; the movement of waste from the colon and sweat pores; the movement of nutrients to the organs, the movement of the blood circulating in our bodies, the movement of our limbs, and even the mother's ability to push the baby out of the womb are all governed by vata. When vata is in a state of balance, it gives us good movement, creative and cognitive skills and public speaking skills. But when it is in a state of imbalance, it causes dry and rough skin, frizzy hair, joint disorders, osteoporosis, brittle bones, arthritis, body aches and pains, bloating, indigestion, flatulence, dry colon and colon-related issues like constipation and irritable bowel syndrome, as well as excessive thoughts, restlessness and anxiety.

Also, have you ever said to your partner, 'Give me some space?' That space in our minds and emotions is where silence, bliss and intellectual capabilities exist. Space is a state of vacuum that we create through meditation practices. In Ayurveda, vata is responsible for our mental faculties and governs our mental space and health. Imbalance in vata often leads to symptoms of anxiety, stress and depression.

5 Elements →3 Doshas

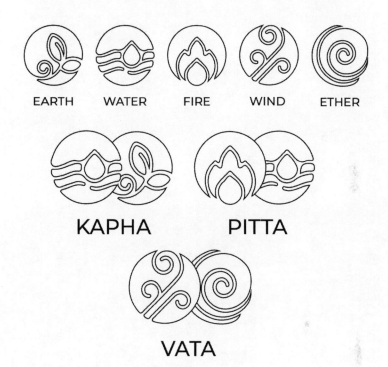

EARTH   WATER   FIRE   WIND   ETHER

KAPHA   **PITTA**

VATA

Your unique biological blueprint

The three biological building blocks in permutations and combinations make seven unique body types, which is called prakriti, or nature of the body, in Ayurveda. All of us have a unique biological blueprint, fixed at the time of conception, and it never changes. We have all five elements and three biological building blocks, but the dominance of one or two biological building blocks determines your body type.

You can find out your unique body type by taking the prakriti quiz below. Check the boxes that best describe you and

FIND YOUR AYURVEDIC BODY TYPE – UNIQUE BIOLOGICAL BLUE PRINT

Check boxes that's applicable for you and tally the count at the end to determine your unique body type – which can be single body type / dual / tridoshic body type.

Characteristics	Vata (Ectomorph)	Pitta (Mesomoprh)	Kapha (Endomorph)
Body Frame	Lean	Medium	Well built
Type of hair	Dry, rough, frizzy	Normal, thin hair, usually straight, prone to hairfall	Voluminous hair, greasy scalp
Colour of hair	Pale, shades of light brown	Red, dark brown, black	Jet black
Skin	Dry, rough skin, easily dehydrates, prone to pigmentation and discoloration	Supple skin, oily T-zone, prone to acne, psoriasis, eczema, urticaria, prone to excess sweating	Moist, greasy skin, soft and healthy
Body weight	Low, struggles to put on weight, tends to lose weight easily	Medium, can easily put on or lose weight, tend to fluctuate easily	Overweight, can put on weight easily, struggles to lose weight
Nails	Blackish, small, brittle	Reddish, small	Pinkish, big, smooth
Size and colour of teeth	Usually very big or very small teeth, tends to chip easily	Medium sized, yellowish	Large shinning, healthy, white teeth
Pace of performing work	Fast paced, always in a hurry, sometimes hyper ventilates	Medium paced, energetic, focused, will complete a task before moving to another	Slow, steady, purposeful, doesn't like to be rushed
Mental activity	Quick, restless, tends to overthink, get anxious quickly, changes mind often	Smart, intellect, aggressive, structured	Calm, stable, doesn't change mind easily
Memory	Short term memory	Good memory	Long term memory

Grasping power	Grasps quickly but not completely, and tends to forget soon	Grasps quickly but not completely, and has a good memory	Good memory
Sleep pattern	Interrupted, restless, tends to sleep less	Moderate sleep hours, sleeps deep and for fewer hours	Sleepy, tends to sleep more, and gets lazy quickly
Intolerance to weather conditions	Aversion to cold temperature, has cold extremeties (feet and hands get cold soon)	Aversion to heat, gets hot quickly, steam and sauna aggravates them	Aversion to moist, rainy and cool weather, inclination towards cold, cough
Reaction under adverse situations	Gets anxious easily, worries, becomes irritable	Gets angry quickly, prone to agression	Calm, reclusive, sometimes depressed
Mood	Changes quickly and has frequent mood swings	Changes slowly	Stable
Eating habit	Eats quickly, without chewing properly	Eats at a moderate speed	Chews food properly
Hunger	Irregular appetite, gets hungry at odd hours	Sudden and sharp hunger pangs, if not satiated leads to headaches	Can skip any meal easily
Body Temparature	Less than normal	More than normal	Normal
Joints	Dry and weak joints, noisy on movement	Healthy with optimum strength	Heavy weight bearing
Nature	Timid, gets jealous easily	Egoistic, fearless nature	Forgiving, grateful, not greedy

Body Energy	Becomes low in evening, fatigue after work	Moderate, gets tired after medium work	Excellent energy, does not get tired easily
Eyeball	Unsteady, restless eye	Focussed, moves slowly	Steady, restful gaze
Quality Of voice	Rough with broken words	Fast, public speaker,	Soft and deep
Dreams	Often has light dreams about the sky, wind, flying objects, confusion, falling from height	Often has bright dreams of fire, light, bright colours, and violence	Often dreams of water, pools, family, and good relationships
Social Relations	Makes less friends, prefers solitude	Good number of friends and socially active	Loves to socialize, makes long lasting relationships
Wealth	Spends without thinking much	Saves but spends on valuable things	Prefers to save more
Bowel Movements	Dry, hard, scanty, blackish stools, prone to constipation, painful bowel movements	Soft, yellowish, loose stools, prone to diarrhoea	Heavy, thick, sticky stools with mucus
Walking Pace	Quick, fast and long steps	Average, steady pace of	Slow with short steps
Communication Skills	Fast, irrelevant, unclear speech	Good speaker with genuine argumentative skills	Authoritative, firm and little speech

your symptoms, and then tally your score. If you have maximum checks for vata, you are a vata-dominant body type and so on. You could also be a dual body type or a *tridoshic* body type. However, do remember that the quiz below may only be partially correct for some of you, especially if you have underlying symptoms. It is advisable to get at least one Ayurvedic consultation done in your lifetime to identify your unique body type with the help of an experienced doctor. It is like identifying your blood type, for which you need professional assistance.

Once you have identified your unique body type, you can personalize your diet and lifestyle based on the tools provided in this book.

AYURVEDIC BODY TYPES

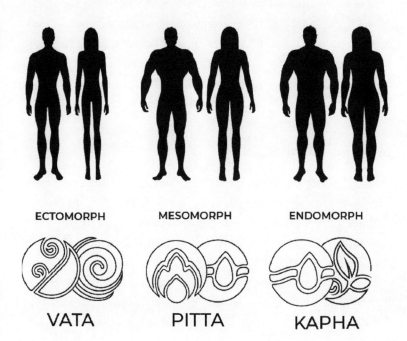

ECTOMORPH   MESOMORPH   ENDOMORPH

VATA   PITTA   KAPHA

Ectomorph, vata prakriti

Air and space elements are more dominant in this body type. The Ayurvedic qualities are cold, light, dry, rough, flowing and spacious. Vata prakriti or ectomorph body types usually have a small frame, thin, brittle bones, an inclination to dryness in their skin and hair, colon health issues like constipation, and bone-related ailments. Since vata governs our thoughts, vata-dominant people are also creative, quick, energetic, flexible, always on the move and thinking of the next big thing. They get bored easily if they're in one place for a long time. They naturally make good artists, designers, musicians, athletes and dancers. They can learn quickly, are naturally good at multitasking and are kind-hearted by nature. However, they can be forgetful, get anxious, distracted and overwhelmed easily, and experience mood swings. They are very sensitive to cold weather, have trouble sleeping, have poor blood circulation, experience irregular appetite or eating disorders, and are prone to digestive issues such as bloating and gas. Those with a vata-dominant personality must have a fixed waking and sleeping cycle, include more grounding workouts in the morning, and aid their digestion with infused teas and water.

Mesomorph, pitta prakriti

Fire and water elements are more dominant in this body type. The Ayurvedic qualities are: hot, light, sharp, oily, liquid and mobile. Pitta prakriti or mesomorph body types usually have a medium frame and an athletic body, with a tendency to gain and lose weight quickly. They have sharp, penetrating eyes and a sharp jawline. Mentally, pitta types are ambitious, hard-working, highly motivated, goal-oriented, competitive and adventurous, self-determined, purposeful, intelligent and known for their tenacious personalities. Their aggressive nature can be off-putting to some people, which can lead to conflicts. They're focused and like to complete one task before starting another. They are strong leaders who do well in management, and they make excellent public speakers. They have very organized minds and work on a schedule. They are able to follow through with tasks, no matter how much effort it takes, and can master new skills easily. They have a quick metabolism, good circulation and healthy skin and hair when their diet is in balance. In a state of imbalance, pitta-dominant people become impatient, experience hunger pangs, mood swings, experience sensitivity to hot temperatures, and are prone to inflammation, abdominal distention and acne, psoriasis, eczema, rosacea, urticaria and other skin disorders. Those with a pitta-dominant personality should focus on work-life balance, avoid extreme heat in the form of excessive steam and saunas, and stay away from spicy and oily foods.

Endomorph, kapha prakriti

Earth and water elements are more dominant in this body type. The Ayurvedic qualities are steady, stable, heavy, slow, cold and soft. Kapha prakriti or endomorph body types usually have a large, stocky frame and thick bones; they tend to gain weight and they struggle to lose weight. They usually have good skin and hair, and their teeth are strong and very well-formed. Their pulse is slow and steady. They love to sleep, have a moderate or low appetite and their digestion is very slow. They enjoy eating gourmet foods that taste and smell good. Mentally, kapha types have a good temperament and are empathetic by nature. They're known for keeping things together, rarely getting upset and thinking before acting. They go through life in a slow and deliberate manner and are a good support system for others. They are kind, caring, trusting, dependable, patient, calm, wise, happy and romantic by nature. They have a healthy immune system and strong bones and joints. However, they can be social recluses and tend to isolate often. They need regular motivation and encouragement to stay focused on their health. When in a state of imbalance, they experience a slow metabolism, sluggishness, a higher risk of heart disease, cholesterol, obesity, mucus build-up, breathing issues (i.e., asthma, allergies), and susceptibility to depression. For good health, a kapha-dominant person should focus on regular exercise and a healthy diet; they must maintain a warm body temperature (e.g., by sitting in a sauna or eating warm foods) and establish a regular and fixed sleep routine.

You could also be a dual body type: vata-pitta dominant, kapha-vata dominant, or pitta-kapha dominant, where you borrow individual qualities from both body types.

Tridoshic

The seventh body type is tridoshic, where all three doshas are in a state of balance. This is considered one of the best body types, as all three biological building blocks are in a state of balance. Kapha is considered the second-best body type due to its ability to build new tissues and faster recovery. Vata and dual body types usually face more challenges, but with a disciplined diet and lifestyle, they can maintain good health.

Three pillars of good health

Ayurveda states that the three pillars of good health are: nutrition (personalized to your unique body type), exercise and sound sleep. When even one pillar is compromised for another, it causes imbalances and affects the overall well-being of a person.

One man's nutrition is another man's poison

Ayurveda offers guidelines on how to eat and what tastes to incorporate in your diet as per your unique body type, so you can maintain balance in your elements. All food groups have a unique prakriti and demonstrate the dominance of different elements. There are six primary tastes in nature: sweet, sour, salty, bitter, pungent and astringent.

Understanding the six tastes and the roles they play in our bodies

Sweet taste is dominant in earth and water elements and is found in wheat, rice, maize, grains, millets, sweet potatoes, milk and sweet fruits. These foods help build new tissues and calm the nervous system. In case of obesity and weight gain, we avoid sweet foods in our diet.

Sour taste is dominant in the fire and earth elements and is found in tangerines, lemons, tomatoes, yoghurt and fermented foods. These foods help in cleansing the tissues and aid in the absorption of minerals from foods. Just like how lemon helps cleanse a greasy dish, the sour taste helps cleanse our tissues too. It also increases the permeability of the gut wall and allows nutrients to pass through them. But in the case of leaky gut syndrome, avoid all sour foods as it causes bigger gaps to be formed in the gut walls.

Salty taste is dominant in the fire and water elements and is naturally present in table salts and sea vegetables. It helps stimulate saliva and digestive juices by improving the taste of food. In case of dryness in the system, introduce salty foods in your diet in the form of lemonade with a pinch of salt, or a salad with some table salt sprinkled on it, to hydrate and lubricate the system from within. Remember one gram of salt retains ten grams of water. In the event of water retention and swelling in the body, reduce the amount of salt intake.

Astringent taste is dominant in the air and space elements and is found in legumes, vegetables, herbs, and fruits such as apples, berries and cherries. It helps tighten the collagen and tissues, absorb excess moisture in our bodies, reverse the ageing process and delay the onset of wrinkles. Berries and cherries are also rich sources of antioxidants, which help reduce oxidative stress in our bodies. It also helps lose weight. Avoid astringent foods in case of body aches and excessive dryness in the system and skin.

Pungent taste is dominant in the fire and air elements and is found in chillies, warm spices, pepper, garlic, onion and radish. These foods have a sharp nature, causing our eyes and nose to water. They stimulate saliva, digestion and metabolism. Pungent and spicy foods aid weight loss. But avoid these foods when experiencing symptoms of reflux, hyperacidity, burning sensation, redness in the eyes, excessive sweating, piles and bleeding disorders.

Bitter taste is dominant in the air and space elements and is found in leafy greens, spinach, celery, cilantro, curry leaves, moringa, fenugreek, carom seeds and herbs. These foods help in detoxifying and deworming the body. Just like us, parasites and worms dislike the bitter taste, so they get flushed out of our system. Bitter gourd is considered one of the best bitter-tasting vegetables that helps purify the blood and improve the health of diabetic patients. Avoid bitter taste in the event of body aches and pains alone.

Now, each taste has a prakriti (personality) of its own. Sweet is earth and water dominant, sour is fire and earth dominant, salty is water and earth dominant, pungent is fire and air dominant, and bitter and astringent are air and space dominant. Using this, Ayurveda arrives at a personalized diet plan for your body type.

Vata dietary plan

A vata (ectomorph) body type is dominant in the air and space elements. So, they must consume foods that are earth, water and fire dominant in order to balance their bodies. They should eat more sweet, sour and salty foods and limit bitter, astringent and pungent foods from their diets.

Vata prakriti usually have weak metabolic fire and sensitive digestive systems, prone to bloating, gases, indigestion and constipation. Ensure your meals are well cooked, warm, moist and greasy with good fats. Avoid raw salads, uncooked foods, cool foods and foods that aggravate the dryness. Incorporate good fats such as ghee, sesame oil, olive oil, avocado oil, coconut oil, almond oil or nut butters into your diet to lubricate the GI tract, allow smooth movement of food and easy elimination of waste. Use the same oils for a full-body self-massage. Limit flaxseed oil in your diet, as it goes rancid and dries very quickly when exposed to heat, oxygen and light.

Incorporate more sweet, sour and salty foods into your diet in the form of stewed fruits and well-cooked vegetables. Stewed fruits can include apples and pears with warm spices such as cinnamon, clove and pepper; sweet fruits such as coconut, avocado, melons, mangoes, papaya, peaches, pineapple, plums, ripe berries, cherries, strawberries and grapes; and some sour fruits such as kiwi, lemons, limes, oranges and grapefruit; fresh dates and figs, apricots, soaked prunes and raisins. Consume well-cooked vegetables such as carrots, beetroot, French beans, sweet peas, asparagus, baked sweet potatoes and avocado; juicy vegetables such as cucumber, zucchini, pumpkin, black olives and winter and summer squash; and greens such as fennel, leeks, okra, parsnip and cilantro.

Due to their low metabolic fire, vata or ectomorph body types usually struggle with bloating from grains, legumes, beans and pulses. Make sure to pre-soak all of them for four to twelve hours in order to dissolve the phytic acid, break down the complex structure and aid digestion. Add a pinch of asafoetida when cooking lentils to aid digestion and release gases. Include well-cooked grains such as amaranth, oats, quinoa, rice, whole wheat, brown rice and white rice; noodles and pasta made of rice; whole wheat or millets; spelt, seitan, sprouted wheat and sourdough bread. Consume more red lentils, mung beans and mung dal. To stimulate digestion, you can also incorporate carminative spices such as cumin, coriander, fennel and carrom seeds; to stimulate the metabolic fire, include warm and pungent spices such as turmeric, cinnamon, cardamom, clove, star anise, fresh ginger, bay leaf, black pepper, mustard seeds and nutmeg.

Vata body types can consume good-fat dairy products (sourced from a cruelty-free cow farm), like organic whole-fat milk, butter, buttermilk, cottage cheese, ghee, yoghurt or curd. Make sure to consume only warm milk, and you can add to it spices like turmeric, nutmeg and cinnamon to keep your body warm. Include pre-soaked and peeled nuts like almonds, peanuts, cashews, coconut, hazelnuts, Brazil nuts, macadamia nuts, pecans, pine nuts, pistachios, walnuts and filberts in moderation. You can also add pre-soaked seeds—chia, flax, pumpkin, sesame and sunflower—or even tahini to your salads. Vata prakriti naturally like sweeteners, which helps them calm down. Include sweeteners like raw honey, jaggery, stevia, monk fruit, rice syrup, maple syrup and molasses.

Foods to limit for vata body type

Limit sour fruits like kiwi, lemons, limes, oranges and tangerines if you are experiencing body aches and pains, as sour foods aggravate the discomfort in the nervous system. Avoid jackfruit and bananas if you are experiencing constipation. A common misconception people have is that bananas cure constipation. But the truth is, bananas help in the binding of stools and are an excellent cure for diarrhoea, IBS or irregular bowel movements. So if you are constipated, bananas will harden your stools and aggravate your constipation symptoms.

People with vata prakriti must consume less bitter, astringent and pungent foods. Avoid frozen vegetables and raw salads as they aggravate the dryness in the gut. Consume less cruciferous vegetables like broccoli, cauliflower, brussels sprouts, cabbage, celery and artichokes. Limit the consumption of pungent vegetables like green olives, onion, peppers, white potatoes, radish and turnips, and bitter foods such as leafy greens, beet greens and bitter melon; also corn, eggplant, tomatoes, kohlrabi, mushrooms, wheatgrass and uncooked sprouts, as they are difficult to digest. Avoid refined grains and foods that are dry in nature, like dry oats, rye, barley, millets, wheat bran, buckwheat, oat bran, corn, couscous, rice cakes, breads, dry cereals, muesli, granola and crackers. However, to ensure you get enough nutrients from these foods, do incorporate well-cooked and moist millet porridge into your diet at least three times a week.

Consume fewer chickpeas, kidney beans, brown lentils, lima beans, adzuki beans, black beans, black-eyed peas, miso, navy beans, split peas, pinto beans, soya products and tempeh. Also limit the consumption of astringent fruits such as raw apples, raw pears, cranberries, persimmons, pomegranates and watermelon, in particular, as they're naturally diuretic and can cause dryness. These fruits can be stewed or consumed in juice form with a pinch of salt and pepper to help hydrate and hold moisture.

Avoid eating dried fruits such as dates, figs, prunes and raisins, as well as popcorn, powdered milk, cold milk, ice cream, frozen yoghurt, agave, white sugar and refined sugars.

Pitta dietary plan

A pitta (mesomorph) body type is dominant in fire and water elements and must consume foods that are dominant in earth, air and space elements to balance their body. Consume more sweet, bitter and astringent foods; limit sour, salty, oily and pungent-tasting foods.

Naturally sweet and astringent fruits—apples, pears, mango, melons, oranges, pineapple, avocado, coconut, grapes, watermelon, plums, pomegranates, berries, cherries, raisins, figs, dates, apricots and prunes—are excellent for pitta. Almost all vegetables are advisable, including leafy greens like spinach, kale, celery, cilantro, curry leaves, moringa, spirulina, parsley, lettuce, collard greens, and watercress; cruciferous vegetables like cabbage, cauliflower, Brussels sprout, broccoli; juicy vegetables like cucumber, zucchini, sweet potatoes, squash; bitter vegetables like bitter gourd and other vegetables like carrot, beetroot, fennel, green beans, asparagus, okra, parsnips, white potatoes, artichoke, black olives, corn, mushrooms and peas.

People with pitta prakriti can consume more whole grains like amaranth, barley, cooked oats, whole grain pasta, quinoa, whole wheat, barley, couscous, granola and all kinds of rice except brown rice, which is heaty. You can also consume legumes like kidney beans, mung beans, pinto beans, split peas, adzuki beans, black beans, black-eyed peas and garbanzo beans. Include only plant-based milk or cruelty-free dairy products—milk, butter, cottage cheese and buttermilk—in your diet. However, avoid consuming ice-cream, cold milk, aged cheese and yoghurt. Pitta has an active and sometimes high metabolic fire, and overnight fermented foods like yoghurt aggravate stomach heat. Meanwhile, ice-creams and cold milk bring extremities to the high stomach heat that can cause blistering of the stomach lining.

You can have pre-soaked nuts such as almonds without the skin, coconut, flax seeds, dill seeds, unsalted pumpkin seeds and unsalted sunflower seeds. You can also indulge in caramel popcorn.

Cook your foods with cooling and good fat oils such as cold-pressed coconut oil, avocado oil, olive oil, walnut oil, sunflower oil, flax seed oil and ghee. Go easy on spices and condiments and choose carminative and cooling spices and herbs such as fresh basil, mint, peppermint, fennel, parsley, fresh ginger, coriander, cumin, cardamom, cloves, turmeric, rosewater, saffron and bitter neem. Include sweeteners like maple syrup, fruit sweetener, barley malt syrup, brown rice syrup, fructose, sugarcane juice, sucanat and stevia. You can also consume sea vegetables, aloe vera juice, fruit or vegetable juice, coconut milk, vegetable broth, herbal teas like barley, chamomile, fennel, hibiscus, jasmine, lavender, mint, raspberry and rose petals to keep the body cool and hydrated.

Foods to limit for pitta

Avoid or consume less sour and citric foods such as lime, kiwi, raw mango, persimmons, rhubarb, tamarind, sour berries and cherries. Limit all nightshades like radish, eggplant, garlic, peppers, onions, olives, raw beets, and raw tomatoes, as they can lead to reflux and bloating in pitta. You must also limit refined grains, corn, millet, brown rice and rye; lentils like tur dal (pigeon peas), urad dal (black gram split) and masoor dal (red lentils); tempeh, miso and soya products. Avoid salted nuts and snacks, as they aggravate the burning sensation in pitta. Limit the consumption of almonds with skin, peanuts, pecans, pistachios, walnuts, cashews, Brazil nuts, hazelnuts, macadamia nuts, sesame seeds and tahini, as these are heaty in nature. A pitta prakriti must also avoid cooking food in oils like sesame oil, almond oil, safflower oil, corn oil, peanut oil and vegetable oil, and heaty spices such as cinnamon, chillies, dry basil, oregano, dry ginger, nutmeg, mustard seeds, rosemary, thyme and fenugreek. They should also avoid heaty foods like honey, jaggary, refined sugar and molasses.

Kapha dietary plan

A kapha (endomorph) body type is dominant in earth and water elements and hence must consume foods that are dominant in fire, air, and space elements in order to balance their body. Consume more bitter, astringent and pungent foods; limit sweet, sour and salty foods.

You can eat astringent fruits such as apples, berries, cherries, strawberries, cranberries, dry figs, peaches, pears, pomegranates, prunes, raisins and apricots; grapes, lemons, limes, persimmons and quince in moderation. Kapha body types can consume almost all vegetables, as they aid weight loss due to their bitter and pungent taste. These include leafy greens: spinach, celery, cilantro, curry leaves, leeks, lettuce and artichoke; cruciferous vegetables: cabbage, cauliflower, broccoli and Brussels sprout; and other vegetables: carrot, beetroot, asparagus, bitter gourd, corn, fennel, garlic, green beans, green chillies, mushrooms, mustard greens, okra, onions, parsley, peas, peppers, radishes, summer squash, turnips, watercress, wheatgrass, sprouts and bell peppers.

Consume grains such as amaranth, millets, barley, buckwheat, couscous, corn, granola, oat bran, dry oats, polenta, quinoa, rye and seitan; and you can include legumes such as black beans, white peas, black-eyed peas, chickpeas, lentils, lima beans, mung beans, mung dal, adzuki beans, navy beans, pinto beans, split peas, tempeh, tur dal, white beans and garbanzos. It's best to avoid dairy, but if you must have it, go for low-fat cottage cheese, ghee and salted buttermilk, in moderation.

Cook your foods in non-GMO corn oil, sunflower oil, almond oil and mustard seed oil, and use the same for full-body oil massages once a week. Have pre-soaked almonds, chia seeds, flax seeds, unsalted popcorn, pumpkin and sunflower seeds, and warm carminative spices such as star anise, cumin, coriander, fennel, turmeric, dry ginger, black pepper, ajwain (bishop's weed or carom seeds), cayenne, mustard seed, nutmeg, cardamom, cinnamon, cloves, hing (asafoetida) and mint leaves. Piper longum (pippali) is the best spice for kapha, as it helps reduce symptoms of asthma, bronchitis, and cough and cold. Also, replace refined sugar with raw honey, jaggery, stevia and monk fruit sweetener. You can also consume aloe vera juice, vegetable juice, spiced herbal teas, black tea and coffee in moderation.

Foods to limit for kapha

Limit sweet fruits in your diet: bananas, melons, mangoes, watermelons, avocados, coconut, fresh dates and figs, and sour fruits: grapefruit, kiwi, oranges, pineapple and plums. Also avoid consuming too many juicy vegetables: cucumbers, zucchini, tomatoes, olives, parsnips, pumpkin and winter squash, and limit sweet potatoes and white potatoes in your diet. Reduce your intake of processed and packaged foods like bread, cooked oats, gluten, pasta, rice, wheat and dairy products such as milk, cheese, ice cream, yoghurt and curd. (Curd is a natural probiotic, traditionally prepared at home using curd culture or lemon juice and contains lactobacillus bacterium which is lactic acid bacteria. While yoghurt is pasteurized and fermented with artificial acids by FMCG companies and is an industrial product. It contains live strains of both Lactobacillus bulgaricus bacterium and streptococcus thermophilus.) Consume fewer kidney beans, soya products, tofu, urad dal, miso and canned beans, and limit your intake of Brazil nuts, cashews, coconut, filberts, hazelnuts, macadamia nuts, peanuts, pecans, pine nuts, pistachios, walnuts, sesame seeds and tahini. Avoid cooking your foods with avocado oil, apricot oil, coconut oil, olive oil, primrose oil, safflower oil, sesame oil and walnut oil. Reduce your salt intake and limit the consumption of maple syrup, molasses, rice syrup, sucanat, turbinado and white sugar.

If you have a dual body type, you can compare both diet plans and consume foods based on the imbalance you are experiencing that day. For example, if you are a kapha–pitta dual body type but are experiencing kapha symptoms such as cold and cough, then you should follow the kapha ingredient chart until you recover.

How much should you work out?

Your exercise routine should also be personalized to your unique biological blueprint.

Ectomorph (vata) body type

People with this body type have a thin body frame and brittle bones; they rarely gain weight, are able to lose weight very quickly and have a lot of energy.

If you are an ectomorph, engage in workouts with fast movements like dancing, brisk walks, cycling and swimming. Ensure that at least 20 per cent of your exercise routine includes weight training because it will help increase your bone density. Another workout to include in your regimen is yoga, to build stability, gain flexibility and give your body a feeling of being grounded.

Mesomorph (pitta) body type

Physically, mesomorphs are the type of people who need a good workout. They have a great deal of fire energy within them that needs to be released. They love to physically exhaust their bodies and use their muscles. They are naturally competitive and do well in sports, boot camps, marathons and other athletic endeavours. If you are a pitta body type, you can exercise for long hours as your body can manage heat production easily. Engage in moderate-tovigorous workouts like swimming, climbing, cycling, jogging and team sports.

Endomorph (kapha) body type

People belonging to this body type usually have the largest of all the body types. Physically, they have wide hips and shoulders and thick, wavy hair. They generally have very good stamina, are often overweight and tend to gain weight very easily. They are slow when it comes to physical activity, and they are also very sluggish, lethargic and difficult to motivate. If you are a kapha body type, engage in intense and long workout sessions and try to get past your laziness. Regular exercise is a must for you and can include long-distance running, rowing or jogging.

No matter your body type, the most important thing is to enjoy your workout. It should not feel like a punishment. When you move, you aid digestion, the downward movement of waste, the sweating of toxins, the burning of fat reserves and the stimulation of the organs. When you engage in specific workouts, for example, targeting your belly, you are simply guiding your body to burn and utilize the fat reserves stored here. Exercise to half your body's capacity until you break into a sweat, and make sure to cool down, stretch and hydrate. Do not overdo your workouts either, as too much of a good thing can also prove detrimental to your health. Excessive workouts can trigger vata (movement) and pitta (metabolic fire) related disorders, which can emaciate your tissues and skin from within, accelerate the ageing process, and cause internal damage to your organs.

Steam baths after a good workout also aid in the sweating out of toxins. However, ensure that you cover your head with a wet towel to prevent the body heat from going up to the sensitive areas in the head region, as it can trigger headaches, nausea, a feeling of fatigue, dehydration and even a short temper. In Ayurveda, this is called *Swedana*, where a patient is made to sit in a steam box that closes around the neck, with the head outside the box.

Deep rest

Just as movement is important for your well-being, you must also ensure that you rest. Resting has probably become the most neglected ritual in our modern lives, to the point where we feel guilty when we rest. It is almost like being caught in a rat race, where even in our state of sleep, we are restless. It is important to sleep deeply so your body can repair and rejuvenate damaged tissues, muscles and nerves and reset your body for a new day. Poor sleep habits can impact your overall well-being at physical, mental, and emotional levels and can also negatively impact your relationships at work and home.

Resting also includes meditating, and consciously engaging in activities other than your career—such as pottery, gardening, long leisure walks in nature, reading, journaling, stitching, embroidery, painting and playing or listening to music. These activities are meditative in nature and help calm the sympathetic nervous system, which is in 'fight or flight' mode, reduce anxiety, improve focus, ground you and help release pent-up negative energy. Resting activities also help release dopamine and serotonin in your body and improve the quality of your life.

Movement of doshas during our lifespan

The five elements also manage our ageing process.

Building phase: At birth, a baby is in the kapha stage, or building phase, of its life, which is between zero and fourteen years. At this stage, we are building bones, muscles, tissues, teeth, nails and hair. Children need more protein in their diet as they are building their bodies and growing taller. Irrespective of their unique body types, most children will experience kapha symptoms like colds, coughs, sinusitis, allergies, asthma, hay fever, lung congestion and bronchial disorders more often.

Transformative phase: Between puberty and menopause, or from the ages of fourteen to forty, we are in the pitta stage of our lives, also called the transformative phase, where we are growing into our unique personalities and transforming our dreams into reality. Predominantly, teenagers and young adults experience pitta symptoms in the form of pimples, acne, sensitive skin, burning sensation and excessive sweating. They are more adventurous and ambitious at this stage of life.

Degenerative phase: After the age of forty, or menopause in women, vata sets in, which is also called the degenerative phase of life. Our bones, muscles and tissues start emaciating slowly. In this stage, we predominantly experience vata symptoms such as dryness in our bodies, colon health issues, bone-related disorders and body aches and pains.

But by investing in our health early and following a disciplined diet and lifestyle based on our unique body type, we can reverse diseases and delay the ageing process.

Age-reversal secrets

By removing impurities and toxins that trigger physical degeneration in your body, and with the right diet, you can turn old cells into new ones. This is called *kaya kalpa* practice in Ayurveda, which is an age-reversal process. We will discuss some of the tools that help preserve health in the coming chapters.

Doshas and the planet

Nature has a peculiar and rhythmic way of functioning. The five elements also play a dominant role in different parts of the planet and govern the topography and vegetation of a place. The earth and water elements are dominant in coastal cities and beaches, and this also has an impact on your health and your life. You will also slow down and experience calmness, heaviness and laziness in your body. Consume locally grown foods in the form of tender coconut water, lemonade, fresh fruits and vegetables to introduce the local bacteria to your gut. Your digestion is slow, and you will find yourself taking more afternoon naps.

In the mountains, you will experience a heightened sense of consciousness and can meditate easily. At a higher altitude, air and space become more dominant, which is why sages and monks often travel up to the mountains to accelerate their spiritual journey. We experience symptoms such as dry and rough skin, frizzy hair and light-headedness. Locals living here should consume more grounding foods—sweet potatoes, avocados, root vegetables—as well as greasy foods to lubricate and moisturize the system from within.

In dry regions, like the Middle East, fire is more dominant. You will experience dehydration, a burning sensation and sensitive skin, and the body reacts sharply to oily and spicy foods. In such a fiery environment, it's advisable to consume cooling foods such as tender coconut water, watermelon juice, cucumbers, fresh dates and sugarcane to sweeten your body.

Doshas around the clock

At different times of the day, different elements play a dominant role. As per the Ayurveda Energy Clock, air and space elements become dominant between 2 a.m. and 6 a.m., and again between 2 p.m. and 6 p.m. Earth and water become dominant between 6 a.m. and 10 a.m. and again between 6 p.m. and 10 p.m. Fire becomes dominant between 10 a.m. and 2 p.m., and again between 10 p.m. and 2 a.m. *(See Chapter 6 for a more detailed explanation.)*

Doshas and their dominance in our bodies

Kapha (earth and water) is dominant in the top part of the body, and the lungs are called the seat of kapha.

Pitta (fire) is dominant in the middle part of the body, and the liver is called the seat of pitta.

Vata (air and space) is dominant in the lower part of the body, and the colon is called the seat of vata.

When any element goes out of balance, it causes symptoms and discomfort in the related part of the body. In fact, pitta (fire) and vata (air) dominate the gut region.

Doshas during seasons

During fall and winter, we experience the vata season. Air and space become dominant, causing the weather to be cold and dry. During summer, we experience pitta season, when fire becomes more dominant, causing hot weather. During winter and early spring, we experience the kapha season. Due to the dominance of the earth and water elements, the weather feels cold and wet.

Ayurveda for gut health

Ayurveda offers a personalized diet for your gut health, taking into consideration all of these elements: your unique biological blueprint (prakriti), your age, gender, phase of life (vata, pitta or kapha phases of life), genetic history, topographic conditions of the city you live in, seasonal changes and the symptoms you are experiencing.

We are all just going home

One of the most powerful lessons I learned in the countryside was:

We come from nature, we go back to nature

When our time on this planet is over, we will dissolve back into earth. We bring nothing with us and we take nothing with us. Yet, all our time on earth is spent accumulating materialistic wealth—homes, cars and investments, diseases and then more diseases. We live as if we are never going to die, and we die as if we had never lived. Despite being born into a marvellous body, engineered to perfection, we end our journey with a body that is riddled with diseases. Despite living in our bodies for so many years, we are not been able to understand or master our bodies. We spend all our time on external activities, knowing that the disciplined time we invest in our careers and our crafts will make us masters of them. Then, with time and experience, shouldn't we have mastered this body too? Shouldn't we have already learned the characteristics of this unique body, what nourishes it, what poisons it, and how to protect our bodies from cellular damage? Shouldn't we actually be getting healthier, stronger and wiser with age?

One can present a medical argument for it saying that oxidative stress, glycation, telomere shortening, side-effects, mutations, aggregation of proteins and natural disasters trigger the ageing process of the gross body. But this is where natural sciences such as Ayurveda and yoga differ. Yoga has proven techniques and tools that help lengthen the telomere, and Ayurveda has panchakarma treatments and kaya kalp, a technique to reverse the ageing process by removing toxins from the body that cause the cells to die. Some yogis have lived up to 100 years and never aged a day. In fact, most of them looked better with age and during their last moments, they were able to experience a blissful exit from their physical bodies through a meditative state or *samadhi*.

Dis-connecting from Mother Nature leads to dis-ease

In the forthcoming chapters, I will share with you a powerful five-step process that has helped thousands of our patients and students around the world heal their bodies.

1. Ayurvedic Energy Clock
2. Food Pyramid
3. Food Chemistry
4. Digestion Period of Foods
5. Lifestyle-Changing Habits

Understanding and implementing the concepts in the following five chapters will help you plug back into Mother Nature. These tools have been derived from Ayurvedic science and are backed by modern evidence-based science. Let the healing begin.

6

The Ayurvedic Energy Clock

There was a time when I hit the cross-fit box five times a week, practised yoga and did pilates four times a week, and even enrolled for aerial yoga, hoop yoga, pole yoga and football lessons. I worked hard, did burpees that felt like death, lifted weights, did box jumps, kettlebell workouts, rope climbs, rowing, cardio, and all the other combinations that they had to offer. I was competitive, and during the high-intensity metabolic conditioning workouts, my only goal was to beat the others at their timing. My dinners were late because I would eat after the workouts. As a result, I slept late and woke up late around 7.30 a.m. or 8 a.m. I made some good friends, had an active social life and was in the best shape of my life.

But, in a few months, I started experiencing a severe burning sensation in my throat that no amount of water could quell, low blood pressure (BP), blackouts and skin issues cropped up again. After a few months, my BP became so low that I was asked by my Ayurvedic doctor to completely stop working out for a few weeks. The excessive exercise had triggered high vata (movement-related) and pitta (fire-related) imbalances in the body due to repeatedly doing healthy rituals at the wrong time. I felt defeated.

Have you ever found yourself in such a situation? Where you did everything right, and yet it backfired on you. I have heard so many of my clients complain that they feel bloated despite eating clean, exhausted and low on energy despite eight hours of sleep and that they followed every possible diet there was and worked hard at the gym, and yet the number on the weighing scale went up instead of down.

Do you know what you and I were doing wrong? Instead of working *with* the body, we were working *against* its inherent nature and breaking it. Sometimes, doing the 'right thing at the wrong time' can be as injurious to your health as doing the wrong things. In this situation, the body's defence mechanism causes it to collect fat because it is preparing for a sudden sickness. And when you consistently ignore what your body is telling you, one day it will stop communicating with you.

This is where the circadian rhythm can help us heal the body. I understood how powerful this tool was when I lived in the countryside, and it helped cure my chronic insomnia.

The circadian rhythm is our natural sleep–wake cycle, which controls the physical, mental, and behavioural changes in the body. It is our body's internal clock, and it governs all organ functions.

Rise with the sun and set with the sun.

We human beings are diurnal. Our body clock directly corresponds to the position and movements of the sun.

Similarly, Mother Nature or the universe has its clock that governs the movement of the sun, moon, planets and seasons and has a subsequent impact on the topography, flora, fauna and human body.

When we sync our internal clock to that of Mother Nature, we can tap into a powerful clock called the 'Ayurvedic energy clock', which can heal us, keep us in good health and even help manifest all our desires!

Ayurvedic energy clock

In Ayurveda, a day is divided into six parts of four hours each, and each part has an optimal activity suitable for it. The Ayurvedic energy clock studies the movement of the sun and moon and how the five elements in nature shift dominance in response to this movement, causing a subsequent impact on the human body.

The six parts in which a day is divided are as follows:

Vata energy clock: 2 a.m. to 6 a.m.

The time from 2 a.m. to 6 a.m. is called the hours of creation. During this time, the earth and the large ocean bodies are resting, and the sun is not visible. The earth, water and fire elements are also at rest. Air and space are dominant in nature, as they blow sweetly and quietly over cities, farms, mountains and lakes alike. This period is also called the vata energy clock.

Vata is the Ayurvedic biological building block in our bodies responsible for the movement of our thoughts, internal organs, food, nutrients, waste and motor abilities. During this period, our organs start waking up and actively eliminating toxins, sending them towards the colon, kidneys and surface of the skin. We start shifting in our sleep and have active and vivid dreams.

Vata is also a subtle energy, or life force, that moves through our bodies. As per Ayurveda, there are five different types of vata energy in our bodies: prana vata, udana vata, vyana vata, samana vata and apana vata.

Prana vata: This is the life force flowing from the cranium down to the rest of the body. Prana means life and vata is movement. The cranium comprises the bones that form the head region, surrounding the brain, eye sockets, nose, cheek, jaw and other parts of the face. Prana vata primarily governs the functions of the brain, lungs and heart. This energy is vital and keeps all living beings alive.

Udana vata: This is the subtle upward-moving life force, which moves from the navel to the heart, lungs, throat and brain. It governs our breathing and takes care of the chest region. Udana vata is responsible for exhalation and the outward movement of energy from the respiratory system and governs our thoughts and speech too.

Vyana vata: This life force governs all circulatory movements originating from the heart to the rest of the body and back. It's the life force that pumps oxygenated blood from the heart to different organs and takes impure blood from all the organs back to the heart. It is an involuntary action and cannot be controlled from the outside.

Samana vata: This is the life force that governs the digestive system—the stomach, intestines and liver. It decides what nutrients must be produced in the body, what must be absorbed and assimilated, and what must be eliminated from the body in the form of sweat, semen and urine.

Apana vata: This is the final downward and outward-moving life force. It is located in the colon and the pelvic cavity and governs all movement and absorption of substances or moisture in the colon and the final eliminatory process—excretions from the groin area. It includes the outward movement of stool, urine, semen and menstrual blood.

The vata life force has a waking effect on the organs and the mind. During the vata energy clock (2 a.m. to 6 a.m.), all the organs in the body start to actively detoxify and release toxins that have accumulated and are ready for elimination as soon as you wake up.

The urge to eliminate waste as soon as we wake up is the first sign of good health. But the inability to evacuate waste completely, difficulty or pain in passing stools, constipation, irregularities in the bowel movement, multiple bowel movements, irritable bowel syndrome or the need to urinate frequently at night are signs of poor colon health. The colon becomes the first organ that informs us of early symptoms of disease and our internal body's health.

Kapha energy clock: 6 a.m. to 10 a.m.

The next period in the Ayurvedic energy clock is from 6 a.m. to 10 a.m., and it is called the kapha energy clock. Kapha is the biological building block made of earth and water that provides physical support, structure and form to our bodies. This energy clock allows you to prepare for the day, nourish your body, gather energy and get to work.

When the sun rises, your body's metabolic fire also rises. The best activity at this time is sun gazing to improve communication between our gut and Mother Nature. It helps improve our focus and concentration as well as our absorption of vitamin D, and the body starts receiving signals to produce digestive juices. In school, we learned the *Aditya Hridayam* by heart. It is a powerful prayer to the sun god, who gives life to all elements and creations on this planet. I was told that if I chanted it nine times, looking at the rising sun without blinking, my wishes would come true, and I piously did so. I'm not sure what I wished for as a child, but this ritual returned many years later to help me heal my body.

No matter what body type you have, you should always start your day with 200 ml of warm water to cleanse your digestive system and slowly wake it up. You should definitely not begin your day with caffeine. Drinking caffeine on an empty stomach dries up the gut lining and destroys the gut flora. If you must drink coffee or tea, have it after breakfast or lunch and never after sunset.

Check your tongue. If you notice white discolouration, it's a sign of toxins and undigested food from the gut being deposited on the tongue at night. In this case, do not drink water on an empty stomach. Instead, do oil pulling with sesame oil (not coconut oil, as it has a drying effect on the mouth), gargle with a mixture of warm water, turmeric and salt, and brush your teeth with a bitter organic toothpaste without fluoride in it, and scrape your tongue with a copper or silver tongue cleaner (not a plastic tongue cleaner or toothbrush). If your tongue is pink, it is a sign of good digestive health. In this case, you can drink water without brushing your teeth, which allows good oral bacteria to enter the digestive system and enhance the gut bacteria.

Your first 'drink' determines how you will feel the rest of the day!

Pitta energy clock: 10 a.m. to 2 p.m.

During this phase, the fire element becomes dominant, and our metabolic fire is also at its peak. This is the most productive time of the day. Have the largest meal of the day, plan your work, organize and take action. Start your lunch with a bowl of steamed salad to help alkalize the body. And post-lunch, have probiotics in the form of buttermilk, kombucha, kefir or digestives like a lemon shot. Remember to 'not' workout during this energy clock where pitta, the fire element is already dominant in the body and the sun is at its peak. Working out during this phase will aggravate the metabolic fire, triggering pitta symptoms like burning sensation, acidity, reflux, skin disorders, inflammation, disoriented state of mind and irritability.

Vata energy clock: 2 p.m. to 6 p.m.

During this time, vata (air and space) once again becomes dominant in nature and our bodies. The drop in temperature allows the movement of a cool sea wind to blow over the land, having a soothing effect on people. Similarly, in the body, vata energy or movement gets activated and dominant, leading to the movement of thoughts, ideas, and a heightened sense of creativity. This is the best time to call for team meetings, strategize, brainstorm and solve problems, and it is also a good time to communicate and socialize.

For an evening snack, you could indulge in a small helping of a fruits of slimy nature like peaches, plums, mangoes, pears, papaya, custard apple, wood apple that helps aid smooth bowel movements the next day; or healthy bites like dried nuts, lotus seeds, puffed rice, homemade granola bars, avocado with freshly baked whole grain bread. Remember fruits and fermented foods like yoghurt or curd, must not be consumed after sunset, as they activate the gut flora and affect natural sleep cycles. Have a light dinner before the sun sets—for instance, a bowl of vegetable soup, a steamed salad and some carbohydrates. Avoid eating heavy foods after sunset.

Kapha energy clock: 6 p.m. to 10 p.m.

During this time, kapha (earth and water) becomes dominant and our bodies feel heavier and experience a drop in energy levels. This is the time to slow down, have the smallest meal of the day, go within and analyse the day's events. Do not consume heavy foods after sunset like deep-fried foods, baked dishes, complex carbs, bread and rotis, and large amounts of protein. It's best to consume light foods like soups and steamed vegetables, and if you are still hungry you could include a small cup of rice (white, brown, red or black based on your body constitution). These are easy to digest and will allow your digestive system to wrap up its duties early so you can prepare for sleep. Ensure a three-hour gap between your last meal and bedtime to avoid sleeping with a pile of undigested food in your gut. A late-night meal when undigested, starts fermenting in the gut, and becomes tamasic in nature, which is considered a negative energy in Ayurveda.

Pitta energy clock: 10 p.m. to 2 a.m.

Fire gets dominant during this time, and the liver, which is the seat of pitta, starts to actively detoxify the body. This is the time for deep REM when the brain puts you to sleep so it can actively repair damaged tissues, muscles and nerves. If you sleep late and miss this repair time, your body will feel low on energy and sapped the next day. That is why, after two or three late nights in a row, our bodies refuse to budge and forcibly shut us down. If you habitually sleep late, it triggers the metabolic fire to become active, midnight hunger cravings, compromising your body's resting period, and can impact your immunity, gut health and thus your mental and emotional health in the long run. If you are in the habit of working late nights and don't consciously take time off to rest, then your body will choose a day to rest and shut off, and you will be unable to do things on your own will. Invest consciously in healthy sleep habits and rituals to remain the master of your healthy body.

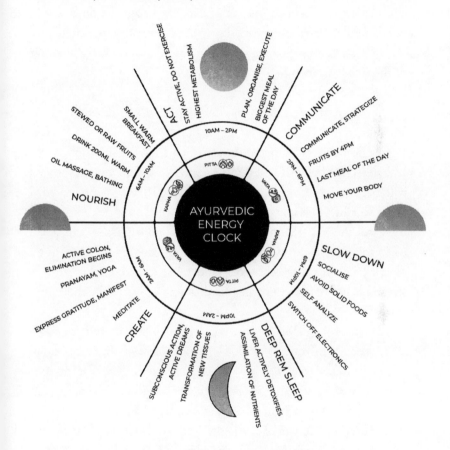

Move your body for a healthy colon

The colon becomes active between 5 a.m. and 7 a.m. and is ready to eliminate waste. Which is why in Ayurveda and many vedic sciences, it is advised we wake up at least forty-five minutes before sunrise. If you miss this clock and are in the habit of waking up late, you will be prone to constipation symptoms as the body's metabolic fire and digestive system become active and the body is focused on receiving new nutrition and digestion rather than eliminating it. Wake up and sit up straight to aid the downward movement of waste. Start your day with 200 ml of warm water and do some stretching, yoga or exercise to aid the smooth evacuation of the waste. Remember:

The parts of the body you don't move attract disease.

If you don't work your core muscles and have a desk job, you will collect belly fat. If you don't exercise your back muscles, they will become weak and the spinal cord will have to carry your body weight. This puts further pressure on your backbone and increases the risk of lumbar health issues. Poor posture can lead to a prolapsed disc and constantly crossing your legs when sitting on a chair can cause the nerves and muscles in both legs to be stretched unevenly, triggering sciatica-related issues in the long run.

To improve colon health, you can incorporate *adho mukha shvanasana* (downward bend), *parsvottanasana* (intense side stretch pose), *bitilasana* (cow pose), *marjari asana* (cat pose), *balasana* (baby pose) and *bhujangasana* (cobra pose) into your yoga practice. The Surya Namaskar is a wonderful set of movements that is a complete workout for the body and the mind. It helps release water retention from the organs caused by excess salt in our diet. It also reduces inflammation, lubricates the joints, muscles and nerves, and aids in the downward movement of toxins. Practise deep stretches such as *ardhamatsyendrasana* (half spinal twist), *supta matsyendrasana* (supine spinal twist), *parivrtta anjaneyasana* (crescent lunge twist), *bhujangasana* (cobra pose), pawanmuktasana (wind relieving pose), *dhanurasana* (bow pose) and *vajrasana* (adamant pose). You can also lie on the floor and place your legs on the wall to improve blood circulation to your stomach region.

Practise pranayama for at least twenty minutes a day. It opens up the chest, improves oxygen supply, strengthens the belly and aids digestion. Breathing exercises such as *kapalbathi* help expel toxins from the lungs.

After a meal, sit in *vajrasan*, if you can, for fifteen to twenty minutes to align your stomach opening with your gut. This facilitates smooth digestion and the downward movement of the food.

Morning workouts vs evening workouts

As per the Ayurvedic energy clock, the morning is considered the most productive time to work out. The energy that is produced in the morning can be utilized throughout the day to pursue your professional and personal goals. When you work out in the morning, you also have an entire day ahead of you to hydrate and nourish yourself at regular intervals. If you work out at night, you barely can drink two or three cups of water and end up dehydrating during your sleep. The excessive dryness in your internal organs causes irritability, which is also a vata imbalance. Post an evening workout, you may even experience restless leg syndrome, active dreams, disturbed sleep patterns and the constant urge to urinate. It's therefore best to work out in the morning, between 6 a.m. and 10 a.m., before the sun and the metabolic fire reach their peak. As mentioned before, the absolute worst time to work out is during the pitta clock of 10 a.m. to 2 p.m. This is when the fire is dominant (the sun); when coupled with your workout, it can double your metabolic fire, causing burning sensations, impaired skin, inflammation, abdominal distention, weak liver and even hair fall.

Type of workouts

Choose your workout regimen carefully. Any movement that is natural and brings you closer to the nature of your own body, such as walking, jogging, yoga, running, cycling, rock climbing, swimming or rowing, is healthy and sustainable in the long run. These are called aerobic exercises, which are low-intensity movements that you can do for a long period of time. These exercises derive energy from nutrients, glycogen and burn fat in the presence of oxygen.

However, with the increase in social pressure to look a certain way, many of us work out muscles that we barely use. For example, bicep curls will give you a great bicep, but you don't perform daily activities, like lifting a shopping bag, with a bicep curl. These exercises are called anaerobic exercises, which you do for a short period of time with high intensity, followed by a period of rest. For example, pull-ups, push-ups, weightlifting and sprinting. These exercises derive energy from the glycogen stored in the muscles in the absence of oxygen, which can help you achieve a desired body shape but will lead to the accumulation of lactic acid and, thus, fatigue in the long run and can accelerate the ageing process. It also leads to a build-up of vata imbalance—drying up of the natural lubricants between joints, muscles and nerves, and burning up of adipose (good fats), which can result in sudden injuries. I have encountered several clients including athletes and models, who religiously did intense workout sessions, but one day had to completely discontinue all forms of exercise following a sudden injury, frozen shoulder, hip immobility, torn ligament and such. Injuries do not happen overnight. It gets built up in the body due to wrong posture, poor alignment, dryness between the joints and muscles, accumulation of lactic acids and vata; and the injury gets triggered when the imbalance is at its peak.

The hour of creation

The 2 a.m. to 6 a.m. vata energy clock also coincides with *Brahma Muhurtha*, which means the hour of creation. It begins one hour and thirty-six minutes before sunrise and lasts for exactly forty-eight minutes.

This is a powerful time for you to visualize and co-create the life you want in partnership with the universe. There is not much traffic or noise in the universe at this time, and you can communicate more clearly about what you need in your life. Express gratitude and do your manifestation exercises at this hour.

Set an alarm to the pleasing sounds of nature, freshen up, preferably wear loose-fitting white clothes, find a clean spot facing the north, east or north-east direction, and sit down in a meditative pose. Allow your brain to rest in a state of zero thoughts. It shouldn't be a struggle. If you have too many thoughts flooding your mind, passively observe them without getting emotionally involved with them. Remember, it's not your baggage to keep. Release it. Download your thoughts by journalling, so it reduces pressure on the brain to remember them.

At this golden hour, your body and mind are also spiritually aligned and connected to the *Akashic* records, which are the libraries of the universe. The Akashic records are considered the universe's way of keeping a record of every single thought that has ever been and will probably ever be. It is like the mystical knowledge held in the astral plane, which is a non-physical plane. Akashic records are said to hold information about our past lives, present lives and even future probabilities that will exist based on our present choices of actions. During this vata energy clock, our mental faculties are at their sharpest and our bodies and minds can download and withstand intense amounts of information from the Akashic records, which can help us make wise decisions and propel our spiritual journey forward.

Intermittent fasting

Intermittent fasting involves switching between fasting and eating on a regular schedule. However, it's important to do it the right way or not do it at all. I have seen many people make the mistake of eating food from 2 p.m. or 3 p.m. all the way up to 10 p.m. or 11 p.m. Allow me to bust some myths. Intermittent fasting doesn't begin after having a seven-course meal late in the night. Intermittent fasting begins at sunset and ends after sunrise.

If you are an endomorph (kapha) body type that tends to put on weight easily and struggles to lose weight, sixteen to eighteen hours of intermittent fasting are recommended.

If you are a mesomorph (pitta) body type that tends to put on weight and lose weight easily, twelve to fourteen hours of intermittent fasting is enough, as you have a high metabolic rate and a tendency to get hunger pangs and headaches.

If you are an ectomorph (vata) body type that tends to lose weight easily and struggles to put on weight, twelve hours of intermittent fasting—between 6 p.m. and 6 a.m.—is enough.

Best time to bathe

Did you know that your bathing habits can also impact your digestion? Your body has a warm energy called metabolic fire or agni. When we have eaten a meal, this energy is focused on the stomach region to aid in the digestion, absorption and assimilation processes. When you take a shower, this energy moves towards the surface of the skin to sweat out toxins through the pores. When you take a shower right after a meal, your body rushes the warm energy towards your skin, impairing the digestive process in the stomach.

Ayurveda recommends that the best time to take a shower is on an empty stomach, early in the morning, after sunrise. You can drink a glass of water before taking a shower, as this hydration helps reduce blood pressure-related issues. Ayurveda recommends using lukewarm or warm water below the heart level to improve blood circulation, and body strength and to keep your agni active, and use room temperature water to wash your face to protect your eyes, nose, ears and mouth (and even hair roots) which are sensitive organs. Hot water bathing is recommended only for senior citizens, children and those who are ill. Cold water dips are a ritual in some countries as a way to boost immunity, better acclimatize to the weather and constrict the blood vessels. However, it is not advisable to do this every day.

Bathing rituals also change based on your body type and symptoms. If you are a pitta body type or have symptoms of liver disorders, indigestion, burning sensation, skin disorders, or acidity; then it is advisable to take cold water baths. If you are a kapha or vata body type that naturally has a cold quality or if you have symptoms of bronchial health issues, cold, cough, allergies, joint disorders, body aches and pains; then it is advisable to take a warm water bath. For those who suffer from neurodegenerative disorders, epilepsy, or nervous health issues; it is advisable to take lukewarm baths.

Bathing rituals can again change based on seasons. During winters, avoid cold water baths as it aggravates kapha and vata imbalances, leading to cold, cough, asthma, bronchial disorders, and accumulation of mucus in the body. During summers, avoid warm water baths as it aggravates pitta symptoms such as bleeding disorders, dizziness, weak digestion, discolouration of the eyes, skin disorders, and excessive sweating.

If you experience inflammation of the muscles, joint pain, soreness, or excess negativity in the mind or body, you can also take a bath with Epsom salt which drains away such negative energy. Many people find soaking feet in Epsom salt calming, as it drains the excess negative energy through the feet and has a grounding effect on the body. In some cultures, salt is placed in small bowls at the entrance of the home, to ward off evil eye or what we call negative vibrational frequencies as salt absorbs moisture and energy around it. Which is why when we take a dip in the ocean, we come out feeling lighter, as the salt in the ocean absorbs excess moisture from our body, reduces water retention, inflammation and soreness.

It is also not advisable to take a bath after sunset because it rushes the blood to the surface of the skin, closes your pores and traps body heat during sleep. You can take a sponge bath if you need to wash away the day's tiredness. Some people are habituated to bathing at night and find it relaxing, but a sponge bath gives you the same calming effect without drying up the skin and weakening immunity in the long run.

Oil massage

Before taking a shower, you can also do a full-body oil massage, which is called *abhyangam* or *sneha basti* in Ayurveda ('sneha' means 'love', and 'basti' means 'pooling of oil'). Use any cold-pressed oils available in your kitchen, such as coconut oil, avocado oil, olive oil, sesame oil, mustard oil, or almond oil and add a little castor oil to this to stimulate blood circulation, reduce body aches and pain, to liquefy fat and lumps with its hot quality. Ayurvedic formulations such as *dhanwantaram thailam, sahacharadi thailam, karpooradi thailam* and *ksheerabala thailam* are very popular. These are rich concoctions of several herbs that help reduce inflammation, pain and swelling in the body, and aid detoxification. Place the oil of your choice in a bowl and place this bowl in hot water to indirectly heat the oil.

A full-body massage with oil improves skin elasticity, lubricates your joints, muscles and nervous system, stimulates blood circulation, moves toxins towards the colon and helps sweat out toxins. You can do a self-massage at least for a few minutes, as often as possible, before taking a warm shower. This will transform your physical, mental, emotional and spiritual health. You can also do a head massage with warm coconut oil or hibiscus hair oil to stimulate hair growth.

You can also do a full-body massage and take a warm shower before taking off on a flight and after landing to counteract the dryness from recycled air. During the dry autumn season, oil massages are a boon for the skin.

Avoid head and body massages when you have symptoms of a cold, cough, sinusitis or fever, or during ailments, periods or immediately after surgery.

Oil massages also help offset vata imbalances. When there is an imbalance in vata, it causes an excess of air and space elements in our bodies, which leads to dryness and roughness in the tissues, bones, muscles and nervous system, triggering neurological disorders, psychosomatic imbalances, colon health issues, dry skin and ageing. Regular oil massages improve longevity and help slow down the ageing process.

Mother of all Ayurvedic therapies—*padha abhyangam* (foot massage)

Our feet connect us to mother earth and help us ground our energies. When you walk barefoot on the earth or grass, it can pull any negative energy out of you that has been causing anxiety and stress. Walking barefoot can reduce your anxiety levels by releasing more endorphins and happiness in your body. Research shows that walking barefoot instead of wearing shoes, also reduces the load on hips and knee joints, and thus reduces the risk of osteoarthritis; and the grounding effects also help reduce pain and improve sleep in the cases of mild Alzheimer's disease.[*][†][‡]

At bedtime, massage your feet with warm sesame oil and ensure to gently press all the points on your soles. This stimulates all the internal organs and helps them begin the detoxifying process. There are 107 *marma* points, or energy centres, in the body, and ten of them are on the soles of your feet and your palms. These ten points are connected to the liver, kidneys, stomach, neck, back of the head, eyes, ears and lower back. Pressing these points improves blood flow to these organs, stimulates detoxification from these organs, reduces anxiety, stress, insomnia, depression, and hypertension and even releases pain from your lower back, easing sciatica and slipped disc issues.

Marma points mean hidden or secret points. They are the junctions between muscles, veins, ligaments, bones and joints. They are also considered the access points to the body, mind and

---

[*] Najia Shakoor, Joel A. Block, 'Walking Barefoot Decreases Loading on the Lower Extremity Joints in Knee Osteoarthritis', *Arthritis & Rheumatology* (2006), https://onlinelibrary.wiley.com/doi/abs/10.1002/art.22123, accessed on June 8, 2023.

[†] Sophie C. Rickard, Mathew P. White, 'Barefoot Walking, Nature Connectedness and Psychological Restoration: the Importance of Stimulating the Sense of Touch for Feeling Closer to the Natural World', *Landscape Research* (2021), https://www.tandfonline.com/doi/abs/10.1080/01426397.2021.1928034, accessed on June 8, 2023.

[‡] Chien-Hung Lin, Shih-Ting Tseng et al, 'Grounding the Body Improves Sleep Quality in Patients with Mild Alzheimer's Disease: A Pilot Study', Healthcare (2022), https://www.mdpi.com/2227-9032/10/3/581, accessed on June 8, 2023.

consciousness. When prana (the source of life) flows freely through the marma points, we experience good health. Eleven marma points are located in our limbs, twenty-six marma points are located in the torso, and thirty-three marma points are located in other parts of the body. They can be activated through regular body massages. Thirty-seven marma points are located in the region, which can be activated through gentle head and neck massages.

In ancient India, kings and warriors wisely used the knowledge of marma points as a self-care tool to recover from the ravages of war.

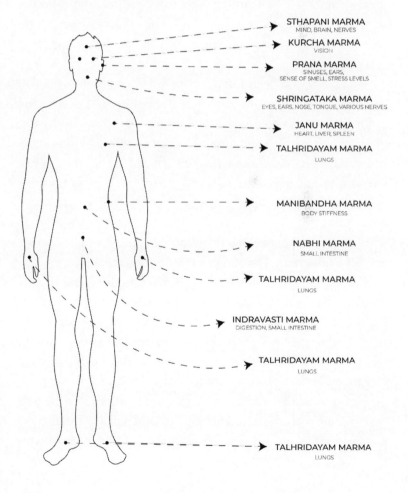

STHAPANI MARMA
MIND, BRAIN, NERVES

KURCHA MARMA
VISION

PRANA MARMA
SINUSES, EARS,
SENSE OF SMELL, STRESS LEVELS

SHRINGATAKA MARMA
EYES, EARS, NOSE, TONGUE, VARIOUS NERVES

JANU MARMA
HEART, LIVER, SPLEEN

TALHRIDAYAM MARMA
LUNGS

MANIBANDHA MARMA
BODY STIFFNESS

NABHI MARMA
SMALL INTESTINE

TALHRIDAYAM MARMA
LUNGS

INDRAVASTI MARMA
DIGESTION, SMALL INTESTINE

TALHRIDAYAM MARMA
LUNGS

TALHRIDAYAM MARMA
LUNGS

Sunbathing

We are nothing but houseplants with complex emotions. Plants need sunlight, without which, no matter how much you water them, they will slowly wither and die. The same is true of our bodies. Without vitamin D, our bodies will struggle to absorb nutrients and other vitamins from the foods we eat. Symptoms such as hair fall, fatigue, body pain, anxiety, stress and depression are associated with a vitamin D3 deficiency. And the best cure for these symptoms is sunbathing. You can get direct sun exposure right after sunrise or just before sunset when the rays are softer on the skin. Make sure to get at least twenty minutes of sun exposure every single day.

Sungazing also helps improve vitamin D3 levels in the body.

Another remedy is to drink sun-charged water. Leave a glass bottle filled with water in the sunlight for four to five hours and then drink from it. It is a great source of vitamin D3. Consume fruits and vegetables like oranges, spinach and mushrooms, grains like oatmeal and organic cereals, and cruelty-free dairy products—milk, yoghurt, buttermilk, cottage cheese, aged cheese, tofu and goat cheese.

One of the biggest culprits for vitamin D3 deficiency is excessive sunscreen. The sunscreen industry has instilled the fear into us that if we don't buy their expensive products and apply a deadly concoction of chemicals to our skin, we will get cancer. To call the life-giving rays of the sun cancerous (instead of addressing the unhealthy dietary and lifestyle patterns with high consumption of carcinogenic foods that trigger diseases from within), is the biggest crime humanity commits against life itself! Vitamin D, or the sunshine vitamin, has been produced on earth for the past 500 million years for free. Our skin absorbs this UVB radiation and converts it into vitamin D3 using the 7-Dehydrocholesterol

(7-DHC) available in the skin. 7-DHC is a pre-vitamin D3 that isomerizes and converts the much-needed vitamin D3 for our bodies. It acts as a cytokine in our bodies, helps fight bacteria and viruses, and prevents osteoporosis, depression, anxiety and even cancer. However, if you are living in countries like Australia, where the ozone layer is thin and has been depleted, you can choose an organic sunblock that is plant-based and devoid of harsh chemicals. In other places, you can use natural sunblocks such as rose water, or wipe your skin with uncooked milk and consume carrot juice as a natural defence mechanism against excess sun exposure.

Most importantly, pay attention to the ingredients in your sunblocks, most of which are known to be endocrine disruptors. Octinoxate in sunscreens is linked to thyroid and metabolic problems and causes allergic reactions to UV light. Homosalate penetrates the skin, disrupts the hormones, and produces toxic breakdown by-products over time that get released in the bloodstream. Some ingredients, such as octisalate, have endocrine effects and bind to oestrogen. Similarly, octocrylene causes skin allergies, disrupts the endocrines and can even cause cancer. Avabenzone can cause allergic reactions and endocrine disruptions and block testosterone in men. Titanium dioxide and zinc oxide, most commonly found in sunblock, have a possible carcinogenic impact and can cause influenza when inhaled. Oxybenzone is also an endocrine disruptor that can lower testosterone in men and increase the risk of breast cancer in women.

Portion your meal based on the position of the sun

When the sun rises, your metabolism also rises, and it grows in direct correlation to the position of the sun. Based on this, it is best to start your day with a small breakfast of a bowl of stewed fruits or warm porridge. Warm foods will stimulate the agni and initiate the digestive system. In the noon hour, the sun is at its peak and your metabolic fire is also at a peak. Have the largest meal of the day during this window. When the sun starts to set, have a small meal again. Completely avoid eating foods after sunset because the body responds to the signal of the setting sun and stops producing digestive juices.

If you have to work night shifts, your diet will have to be altered to include warm spices, which mimic the energy of the sun, and easy-to-digest foods in order to stimulate metabolic fire and digestive juices. You can have a large meal before sunset and after sunrise, and during your night shift, consume smaller meals with warm spices when hungry, so your digestive health still gets to sync with the movement of the sun and rest in the absence of sunlight. And if you are in a country where the days are short and nights are longer, adjust your meal timing and potion of meals based on the position of the sun.

Getting a good night's sleep

For a good night's sleep, make sure to switch off your electronics an hour before bedtime. Don't expose yourself to blue light; don't scroll on the phone; and don't watch Netflix. Instead, read a book. It soothes the fire (pitta) in the eyes, which consumes ten million bits of information per second. With a book, there is only black and white to experience, and the absence of colours or 3D images, relaxes the eyes and allows for the production of melatonin in your body. Melatonin is a powerful hormone that your body produces in response to darkness. It controls your circadian rhythm as well as your waking and sleeping cycles. Do not get habituated to artificial melatonin in the form of medicines, as it weakens the body's natural ability to switch off.

Sleep deeply so you can wake up before the sun and keep repeating this circadian rhythm until it becomes a routine. It will reveal a new you—happier, more energetic and full of life.

Seasonal rituals

These include elaborate changes in the diet, mono dieting, fasting and detoxification, in order to acclimatize to the new season with very few or no episodes of seasonal sickness. The ground rule is:

Eat seasonal, eat local, live global

During the summer season, fire becomes more dominant. Acclimatize by eating foods with cooling energy: watermelon, cucumber, lemonade and muskmelon; astringent foods like watercress, apples and berries; and bitter foods like leafy greens, arugula, spinach and kale. You can include herbs like basil, cilantro and mint in your diet.

During fall and early winter, air and space become dominant, causing the weather to become cold and dry. Consume good-fat foods such as bananas, avocados, cold-pressed oils, as well as spices, warm fluids, ginger and herbs like lemongrass and mint. Avoid raw salads during this season, as they aggravate the dryness inside the body. Instead, include steamed vegetables, whole nuts and nut butter in your diet.

During winter and early spring, earth and water elements become dominant, and the weather turns cold and wet. Eat warm, mildly spiced, well-cooked foods with spices such as turmeric, cinnamon, clove, grated ginger, pepper, star anise, nutmeg, cardamom, carrom seeds, asafoetida, cumin, fennel, lemon, mustard seed, and bay leaves. Also include mung beans, black gram and lentils in your diet. These foods will stimulate metabolic fire and keep the body warm from within. You can also include honey, sesame seeds, and basil to boost your bronchial health.

If you follow this, you will be better able to acclimatize, improve your energy levels, and boost your immunity even against diseases caused by external factors.

7

Food Pyramid: Brickwork to Good Health

Sometimes, no matter how well and cleanly we eat, we experience fatigue. This is because our bodies cannot fully absorb and assimilate the nutrients, so we compensate with high doses of artificial vitamins and supplements, which our bodies still cannot absorb because we haven't addressed the root cause— malabsorption. Our ability to eat and digest food and absorb and assimilate nutrients completely depends on the rhythm we build between our internal clock and Mother Nature.

Once you have understood the internal body clock, the next step is to address the food on your plate and ensure you are eating the right quantity of different food groups.

The 'plant slant'

The best diet in the world that helps address our nutritional deficiencies is the 'plant slant' diet. Ayurveda states that 90–95 per cent of our diet must be plant-based, and 5–10 per cent can be animal-based foods, but these should primarily be cruelty-free dairy products such as milk, yoghurt, buttermilk, cheese and ghee.

In fact, this is also the health secret of people living in the blue zones, which are regions in the world where people live longer than average and have the highest number of centenarians. Okinawa Island in Japan has a food culture that emphasizes the 'plant slant diet' and eating 80 per cent of the appetite. Over 95 per cent of their diet consists of fresh fruits and vegetables, nuts and seeds. They also consume locally sourced fruits and vegetables that are seasonal, pesticide-free and organically grown, such as greens, beetroot, turnip tops, spinach, kale, shards, collards, yams and sweet potatoes. They have at least a quarter pound of fruit per day, which is the size of an apple. And they use good fats like olive oil, which increases good cholesterol and lowers bad cholesterol. They also don't supplement with vitamins, don't count calories and don't weigh their protein. They don't consume packaged foods and are conscious of the quality of ingredients, but at the same time, they do not restrict foods or follow fad diet plans. In fact, they celebrate food! Compared to the rest of the world, they eat:

Equal proportions of carbohydrates, vegetables and very little protein

In Costa Rica, people eat fewer calories, have light dinners early in the evening, and have a traditional Mesoamerican diet of locally available plant-based foods. Loma Linda in California, where the Seventh Day Adventists have a longer life expectancy compared to their neighbouring cities, follow a strict vegetarian diet along with good exercise.

By simply adopting a plant-based diet for some time, you can address all the deficiencies in your body and reverse diseases. Your body is a magical piece of nature. It can heal itself if you feed it nourishing foods instead of foods that deplete prana. All you need to do is simply support the process and not interrupt this intuitive intelligence, which is like intelligent software installed by nature inside of us.

Ayurveda states that 50 per cent of your diet must come from fresh fruits and vegetables that are naturally high in prana. These foods support life, which is also why you'll find a lot of insects, little bugs and butterflies fluttering towards fruits and vegetables rather than towards meat. This is because fruits and vegetables are alive with active microbial enzymes that help enhance your gut bacteria. When we consume natural probiotics in the form of fruits, we are allowing these active microbial enzymes to enter our gut and improve the flora.

Next, 30 per cent of your diet can come from grains, legumes, lentils, nuts and seeds. The level of prana is slightly lower in grains as compared to fruits and vegetables. This is also the reason why fruits and vegetables have a shorter shelf life—they decompose faster.

Ensure that the remaining 20 per cent of your diet includes spices, herbs, condiments, good fat in terms of cold-pressed cooking oils, and plant-based milk or cruelty-free dairy products only if needed. Avoid refined oils, refined sugar, refined flour and refined salt that increase the gap in the gut walls because of their fine quality, triggering leaky gut syndrome. Also, avoid genetically modified foods like GMO wheat in your diet; these are inflammatory, stick to the inside of your gut walls, fermenting causing food intolerances, and further weaken the gut. Either avoid or slowly reduce your intake of dead foods like meat and seafood that have no prana or active microbial enzymes that can aid the digestion process.

The three gunas

There are three types of guna (qualities) in our minds.

Sattva is a state of goodness, calmness and harmony, which is fuelled by freshly cooked foods. A sattvic diet, which is my favourite diet, includes foods that are rich in prana, the source of life. They include fresh fruits and vegetables, juices, wholemeal bread, pulses, grains, sprouts, nuts, seeds, herbs, honey and cruelty-free and hormone-free dairy products. Satvic foods increase your state of awareness and consciousness, inspire positive action and also take you to a deeper sense of meditation. They help unleash your inner potential and creativity. They are foods that are cooked with a lot of love and consumed with awareness and gratitude. Sages, monks and yogis live on a sattvic diet for years and master their bodies, minds and emotions. Sattvic food is based on the principle that you should love all creatures just as you love yourself.

Rajas is a state of passion, activity and movement, which is fuelled by warm spices, spicy and hot foods like capsicum, onion, garlic, radish, black pepper, asafoetida and chillies, coffee, tea, aerated drinks and sugary treats, including chocolates. While they give a stimulating effect and uplift your energy, it is momentary and they can actually give you a low feeling or even increased stress when the effect wears off. The positive aspect is that it gives you leadership skills, like the raja or king who leads his kingdom with good direction, communication skills and ambition. The negative aspect is that it feeds your body at the expense of your mind and breaks your body–mind equilibrium. The ugly part is that, when you consume these foods in excess, it leads to poor digestion and health issues, such as hyperacidity, acid reflux, burning sensations, a short temper and irritability. Consume these kinds of foods in small portions once or fewer times a week.

Tamas is a state of ignorance, inertia and laziness and is responsible for negative emotions like anger, attachment, depression, dependency, self-doubt, guilt, boredom, irritation, addiction, apathy, confusion, grief and ignorance. Foods that contribute to tamas include meat, fish, eggs, poultry, stale food, packaged food with a lot of chemical additives, reheated foods, alcohol, cigarettes and addictive drugs. Even sattvic foods can turn tamasic when they are old, reheated or deep fried. These foods do nothing to uplift your energy and take you down to a state of inertia, heaviness, gluttony, lethargy or aggression. They also reduce your awareness of yourself and those around you, which is why, on important religious occasions, we stay away from tamasic foods.

Back in the day, only warriors ate tamasic foods, like the meat of a dead animal, because it fuelled their aggression and ability to kill the opponent without a moment of sympathy or hesitation. But they would pay a heavy price through imbalances in their minds. Upon returning home to domestic life, they would consciously shift to a sattvic diet to reduce mental aggression, incidences of domestic violence (which stems from a tamasic state of mind), and PTSD which soldiers even today, suffer post-war.

Late-night meals

Meals consumed late at night are considered tamasic in nature because they end up staying in the gut all night due to a lack of digestive fire. The food begins to ferment and rot inside the system, releasing gases and undigested metabolic waste. Imagine keeping food outside the refrigerator overnight—how stale the food would be the next morning and how rotten it would smell. Now imagine that happening inside your system. Seven-course meals, late-night socializing, and late-dinner events have sadly become the bane of our gut health. Overloaded with undigested foods, the gut becomes sluggish and stressed. Quite often, the undigested foods leak into the bloodstream, triggering the body into an auto-immune response. The results are abdominal distention, bloating, constipation, lack of appetite, an inflammatory condition and puffiness around the face and body in general. It is very important to finish your last meal at least three hours before going to bed so the food is completely digested, absorbed and assimilated into the system. Cutting out late-night dinners is a simple trick that can help you reverse belly fat and fix your digestive health, metabolism and weight loss efforts. Don't partake in anything that causes harm to your body, because:

Your body is like the holy grail, temple or any other place of worship in which your spirit lives.

How much carbohydrate and protein should you actually eat?

Ayurveda states that people with a vata (ectomorph) body type, which is the thinnest body type, can consume half a plate of carbohydrates, a quarter plate of protein, and a quarter plate of vegetables, accompanied by good fat to aid digestion. Someone with a pitta (mesomorph) body type, which is a medium build, can consume equal parts carbohydrates, protein and vegetables. And those that are of the kapha (endomorph) body type, which is the thickest body type, must consume half a plate of vegetables, a quarter plate of proteins and a quarter plate of carbohydrates.

Protein and exercise

I meet both female and male professional bodybuilders at our clinic. Most of them come to us with similar imbalances and the most common symptoms they face include chronic constipation, piles, bleeding disorders, acidity, burning sensations in the urinary tract, skin disorders, anxiety and restlessness triggered by heavy workouts, and high creatine levels, sluggish livers and poor kidney functions from the protein overload, which also accelerates the ageing process.

Once, a young man, all of thirty-three, emailed us for a consultation. In his photograph, he had massive biceps, literally the size of a melon. But when he turned on his video, I was shocked to see an emaciated person who was barely one-third the size of the person in the photograph. We found out that he had colon cancer. When I asked his sister if he was on a protein overload, she said the only things he consumed for months together were chicken and whey protein.

We have also seen wrestlers and weightlifters with urinary incontinence and such severe constipation that they have to rush to the hospital every now and then.

But, to my joy, I also met this professional female bodybuilder who worked for the US Air Force. She learned Ayurveda from us and started applying the principles in her bodybuilding journey to make it sustainable and healthy, as opposed to going to extremes and ending up with a fatal impact on her health in the future.

The protein myth!

One of the biggest myths in the industry is that we get protein only from animal-based foods. Then where do cows and herbivores get their proteins from? Plants.

Plants are the first natural and edible source of protein. They're loaded with nutrients, fibre and healthy bacteria, which makes it easier for the human body to digest, absorb and assimilate them, leaving you more energetic and healthier. Animal-based protein has more saturated fats, and foods like meat and fish can take as long as two to three days to fully digest. The proteins and fats they contain are complex molecules that take longer for your body to pull apart.

Besides, animals get cancer and complex diseases just like humans. Plants don't get cancer like animals do. Animals also release cortisol, a stress-based hormone, during confinement, when they are separated from their offspring, and during slaughter. We already live high-stress lives and have elevated cortisol levels—added reasons to stay away from foods such as beef, eggs, casein protein and shellfish.

Higher intakes of animal protein increase the risk of premature death, according to recent studies.[*] The research from National Institute of Health, even showed that 'adults in the 50 to 65 group who reported a high protein intake had a 75 per cent increase in overall mortality and were 4 times more likely to die from cancer during the following 18 years than those in the low protein group'. Those who consumed more meat and protein from animal-based sources increased their risk of death from chronic disease, due to decreased kidney function and increased production of cancer-related hormones. Red meats (beef, lamb and pork) and processed meats (bacon, sausage and deli meats) are metabolized into toxins that cause damage to our blood vessels and other organs. This

---

[*] Carol Torgan, 'Protein Consumption Linked to Longevity', National Institutes of Health (2014), https://www.nih.gov/ news-events/nih-research-matters/protein-consumption-linked- longevity#:~:text=Adults%20in%20the%2050%20to,in%20the%20 low%20protein%20group, accessed on June 8, 2023.

toxic process has been linked to heart disease and diabetes. And most importantly, your plate and stomach are not graveyards for the dead! Live and let live. Remember, the universe (and karma) act like a boomerang. All the positive or negative emotions and actions we create return to us, be it kindness, empathy, love, forgiveness, pain or death.

Nutrient alternatives

Sources of plant-based protein: We have 300 varieties of lentils. Then there is tempeh made from rice, barley or wheat. We also have edamame, chickpeas, peanuts, almonds, spirulina, Burmese tofu made from chickpeas, quinoa, chia seeds, hemp seeds, beans with rice, potatoes, protein-rich vegetables like leafy greens, spinach, kale, mushrooms, broccoli, seitan and Ezekiel bread.

Plant-based amino acids: Quinoa, tofu made from chickpeas, tempeh, edamame, amaranth, buckwheat, Ezekiel bread, spirulina, hemp seeds, chia seeds, nutritional yeast, peanut butter, rice and beans and pita and hummus.

B12 sources for vegetarians: Yoghurt, low-fat milk, plant-based milk, cheese, whole grain cereals that are not processed, nutritional yeast, seaweed, algae, mushrooms, non-dairy milk, breakfast cereals and vegan spreads.

Sources of collagen: Tempeh, tofu made from chickpeas, garlic, citrus fruits, broccoli, tomatoes, leafy greens, kale, spinach, green tea, asparagus, strawberries and chickpeas.

Plant-based Omega-3 fatty acids: Chia seeds, Brussels sprout, algal oil, hemp seeds, walnuts, flaxseed and perilla oil.

Sources of ALA: Chia seeds, walnuts, flax seed oil, Brussels sprout, flax seeds and edible seaweed.

Millets

Ensure you include millet in your diet. Millets are the superfoods in your kitchen. They are gluten-free, starchy grains loaded with nutrients, vitamins and minerals such as calcium, phosphorus, iron, folate, magnesium and amino acids. A porridge made from millets is by far my favourite breakfast; it offers a perfect balance of carbohydrates, proteins and fibre, which provides a continuous flow of energy through the day, satiates hunger, lowers cholesterol, improves colon health and does not create indigestion or gases, unlike other grains. You can simply boil two teaspoons of millet in a bowl of water, add some salt and you are good to go. Include ragi (finger millet), foxtail millet, jowar (sorghum millet), bajra (pearl millet), buckwheat millet (kuttu), amaranth (rajghira), little millet (sama), barnyard millet, broomcorn millet (chena) and kodo millet.

Unfortunately, millets and the farmers growing these crops have been displaced by high-profit, low-nutrient processed cereals, genetically modified refined wheat, soya and corn that feed the pockets of rich FMCG companies but cause more harm to your gut than good. Anything processed with human intervention is stripped of its natural nutrients and takes you away from nature. With every food choice you make, ask yourself, '*Does this food take me closer to nature or away from it?*'

How to drink water

Water is prana, the source of life. Do not drink water from a plastic bottle. Scientists have actually found microplastics in human blood, which are cancerous. This happens when sunlight comes into contact with a plastic bottle, releasing the microplastics into the water instead. Store water in earthen pots after boiling it. You can also drink water out of copper or silver, as it alkalizes the body, or you can drink water out of glass and steel, as they don't leech into the water. Every drop of water has thousands of microorganisms living in it that continue to be born and die in the water. Boiling water eliminates these micro-organisms, bacteria and any parasites and keeps them bacteria-free for a certain number of hours based on the season while retaining the minerals and nutrients in the water.

Ensure to drink adequate water. We once had this young journalist who came to us with symptoms of urine in his blood, which was caused by kidney stones. My doctors were able to exactly point out the lifestyle habits that were causing this—raw salads, lack of hydration and pitta imbalance—which were also contributing to his dehydration and temper issues. We administered him some herbal *ghrutam* (ghee-based) medicine to lubricate and hydrate his gut and increased his water intake. Within two weeks, he sent us a picture of a kidney stone that he passed naturally, without any pain or bleeding.

Also, don't gulp water while standing. Sit down and sip water slowly, because otherwise the water rushes down to the lower belly creating vata imbalances like burps, nausea and cramps, and the body doesn't get time to absorb the nutrients and minerals in the water. It also puts pressure on the kidney and bladder and the impurities—instead of getting flushed out—get deposited there. Long-distance runners, who have to hydrate during the run are advised to take small sips and not gulp water to prevent exercise-associated hyponatremia (EAH). It is a condition where excess water during exercise overwhelms the kidneys and gets absorbed by the cells instead leading to swelling in the body. It also causes the blood sodium levels to drop causing other symptoms like confusion, irritability, fatigue, convulsions, headache, loss of appetite, muscle weakness, spasms, and nausea.

Best times to drink water

Drink 200 ml of warm water as soon as you wake up to cleanse your GI tract and eliminate toxins from the gut. Drink a glass of water before taking a shower to lower your blood pressure and keep your body cool and calm. Drink a glass of water half an hour before every meal, as this cleanses the palate and helps the GI tract prepare your body for the next meal. Do not drink too much water while you're eating food, as it washes away the digestive juices. Drink water thirty minutes after having completed your meal. Also, drink a glass of water at bedtime, as this helps reduce the chances of cardiac arrest.

Remember, water is life. Many scientists tried to show through experiments how water could carry memories, although it remains much debated by their peers. Scientist Jacques Benveniste's showed how water carried memories of the original molecule even when diluted several times. German scientists showed through experiments that water can carry memories and information about all the places it has travelled through, by dipping a flower in water and removing it, and later magnifying the water molecule to find the effect of the flower still visible. Scientist Masaro Emoto demonstrated how positive emotional content created beautiful crystal formations in water when frozen, and negative emotional content generated ugly patterns. While these experiments continue to face much scepticism in the modern-day world, cultures around the world have for thousands of years performed rituals, prayed and chanted to water in temples and churches, to bless their people with the said holy water. Either way, whether you are a believer in science or religion, remember water nourishes your body and sustains life itself. Express gratitude before you eat and drink so your body can receive the nutrients in a positive environment.* †

Infused water recipes

We started introducing our clients to infused water recipes to address their gut health issues. There were several patients who came to us as a last resort for their gut health when, despite several invasive check-ups like colonoscopy, endoscopy, biopsy and blood tests, doctors couldn't identify the problem. Within a few days of changing their water, their health dramatically improved and all symptoms of gastritis, gut dysbiosis, bloating, indigestion and reflux disappeared. My in-house doctors noticed that the patients' dependency on Ayurvedic medicines had also reduced. When you change the water, you are impacting 75 per cent of the human body, which is made of water. And that's what infused waters do—they radically change and improve your health.

I am sharing with you some of my favourite infused water recipes that you can start your day with based on the symptoms you experience.

---

* Yolène Thomas, 'The History of the Memory of Water', *Homeopathy* (2007), https://pubmed.ncbi.nlm.nih.gov/17678810/#:~:text=The%20 idea%20of%20the%20memory,have%20confirmed%20the%20 basic%20results, accessed on June 8, 2023.
† Faculty article, 'Scientists Show That Water Has Memory', Resonance Science Foundation, October 4, 2018, https://www. resonancescience.org/blog/Scientists-Show-That%20Water-Has-Memory#:~:text=The%20German%20scientists%20believe%20 that,that%20it%20has%20been%20on, accessed on June 8, 2023.

For constipation, dry skin, dry lips and hair

If you are an ectomorph (vata) body type, you may have an inclination towards dry and rough skin, constipation and a tendency to lose weight. Start your day with one teaspoon of ghee melted in 200 ml of warm water. You can have plant-based ghee. And if you choose to have dairy-based ghee, ensure it is sourced from a cruelty-free cow farm only. That way, it is devoid of hormones and diseases for you and devoid of cruelty to that animal.

Ghee has butyric acid, which improves digestion, lubricates the GI tract right from your mouth to your stomach, intestines and colon, and helps in eliminating waste smoothly. It has a high concentration of monounsaturated Omega 3, which is great for heart and cardiovascular health, and it has non-inflammatory benefits. It helps reduce dryness caused by vata (air) imbalances and inflammation, reflux, acidity and the burning sensation caused by pitta (fire) imbalances. However, if you are experiencing symptoms of a cold, cough, sinusitis, heaviness or obesity, you must avoid consuming fat on an empty stomach, as it can aggravate these symptoms.

To lose weight and stimulate metabolism

If you are an endomorph (kapha) body type with a heavy frame, a sluggish metabolism and a tendency to gain weight, you can start your day with 200 ml of warm water with the juice of half a lemon, a pinch of cinnamon and grated ginger. This will help boost your metabolic fire. However, avoid these ingredients if you are experiencing a burning sensation, reflux, acidity, GERD or even body aches and pains, as lemon aggravates these symptoms.

Here is another recipe. To 200 ml of water, add one cinnamon stick, one clove, four peppercorns, one cardamom, one teaspoon of grated ginger and some lemongrass, and boil it well. Cinnamon, cardamom, and clove are warm spices that have anti-inflammatory and antioxidant benefits. It helps stimulate the metabolic fire. You can consume this drink after meals to boost your metabolism and digestion. Note, do not consume these ingredients if you have pitta-related symptoms like burning sensations, hyperacidity, acid reflux, skin disorders, fever or diarrhoea. This concoction helps cure colds, cough, sinus allergies and throat infections. Add a portion of apple juice to this along with a slice of tangerine to make a mocktail for the evening, so you can stay away from sugary drinks, and alcohol and still have fun.

For acidity or GERD

If you are a mesomorph (pitta) body type with high metabolic fire, you may have a tendency to put on weight and lose weight easily and an inclination towards symptoms like acidity, reflux, GERD or a burning sensation in your GI tract. Start your day with a teaspoon of holy basil seeds, also called sabja seeds, soaked in a glass of water overnight or for an hour. These seeds will swell up into a jelly-like substance when soaked in water. When consumed on an empty stomach, holy basil seed water has a cooling effect on your stomach and gut. It absorbs the excess stomach acids and washes them down towards the colon and out of your system.

Post lunch, you can have buttermilk made from fresh yoghurt, which is technically salted lassi but also called buttermilk for want of a better word. Do not have yoghurt, curd or even buttermilk after sunset, as it has active bacteria that will affect your sleep cycle and cause a cold and cough (kapha-related symptoms) or skin disorders, GERD, acidity (pitta-related symptoms). Alternatively, you can have sweetened rose syrup added to room-temperature milk after your meal to prevent the stomach acids from rising upwards. And most importantly, sleep on the left side of your body because the oesophagus enters the stomach from the right side. When you lie down on the left side, the oesophageal sphincter lies above the stomach acid levels and prevents the acid from rising upwards.

For indigestion, bloating and gassiness

This is an easy and life-changing recipe, also famously known as 'CCF tea' in Ayurvedic circles. Take 500 ml of water and add to it one teaspoon of cumin seeds, one teaspoon of fennel seeds, and one teaspoon of coriander seeds. At Prana, we also add one cardamom and a small pinch of carrom seeds to this concoction to stimulate the agni and help in deworming the gut. Boil this and bring it down to half. Filter and drink one cup before every meal to boost your digestion and prevent bloating and flatulence. These spices are carminative in nature; they stimulate saliva and digestive juices in your body. It also helps reduce nausea and acidity symptoms by aiding the downward movement of food and fluids.

Cholesterol, high blood pressure, period cramps

If you have been suffering from cholesterol, high blood pressure issues, period cramps, or pimples and acne, it's best to start your day with a bitter drink to purify the blood. Soak one teaspoon of fenugreek seeds (methi seeds) overnight in a glass of water. The next morning, boil the seeds in the same water until it is reduced by half. Strain and sip this warm water. This drink helps lower blood sugar levels, boost testosterone and reduce high oestrogen levels that can cause pimples and acne. It also improves milk production in breastfeeding mothers, reduces cholesterol levels and inflammation, curbs a high appetite and even reduces period cramps. Fenugreek seeds are loaded with vitamin A, vitamin B, vitamin C, iron, phosphorus, potassium and even calcium, which are excellent for your immunity and metabolism.

Addiction: the bane of our existence

Another issue afflicting our health is the addiction to caffeine. At one point in time, I was having coffee instead of lunch at work and ended up with a severe stomach infection that triggered nausea and diarrhoea. My body couldn't hold any food inside, and I even woke up at night to throw up. I was sick for almost ten days, and that event marked another moment of deep learning.

Coffee is the most expensive food commodity in the world. You could buy an exotic coffee digested and pooped by an animal for a few hundred dollars, or one laced with gold. At one point in time, distinguished universities published research on how caffeine is injurious to health, and the World Health Organization included coffee in a list of possible carcinogens in 1991, but in 2016 they retracted the same and replaced it with a statement that there is 'no conclusive evidence for a carcinogenic effect of drinking coffee'. There are controversial reports in California that acrylamide found in coffee (even in potato chips, French fries, toasted bread), is linked to cancer in rats, while peers argue that these research findings cannot be applied to humans. The scientific world is flooded with articles on how coffee is good for health.* †

---

* The Nutrition Source, 'Coffee', Harvard T.H. Chan School of Public Health (article last reviewed on July 2020), https://www.hsph.harvard. edu/nutritionsource/food-features/coffee/, accessed on June 8, 2023.
† The Nutrition Source, 'Coffee Warning Label Conflicts With Public Health Guidance', Harvard T.H. Chan School of Public Health (April 2018), https://www.hsph.harvard.edu/nutritionsource/food-features/ coffee/, accessed on June 8, 2023.

Who stands to profit from this research? Clearly, they're the ones who fund this research to further sales. Quite often, researchers are given predetermined conclusions and asked to provide facts and numbers to arrive at these results.

Either way, here are some reasons why you must hold back that extra cup of coffee. Coffee has a bitter taste, which is actually a natural pesticide the plant releases to ward off predators. Although safe for human consumption, the bitter pesticide continues to have a similar effect on the gut. Initially, it helps release waste, but coffee also strips off the good fats in the digestive system, irritates the gut lining, triggers irritable bowel syndrome and causes you to dash to the bathroom. Many people have become so dependent on this effect that they cannot empty their bowels without having coffee. Coffee also causes dryness in the gut and vata imbalances, which can lead to long-term constipation symptoms that are difficult to treat. According to Ayurveda, excess coffee also depletes your body of ojas, the essence of life, because it triggers an upward (udana vata) and outward (vyana) movement of life force, leaving you emaciated and with a loss of nourishment. When you drink coffee, you are actually living on borrowed energy. Your body utilizes an entire day's energy stock within a few hours. But when this effect wears off, you end up with lower energy levels and thus a cyclical addiction to coffee sets in. Coffee has a similar effect on the brain as alcohol and hard drugs do. It narrows the blood vessels in the brain, which impairs our cognitive abilities, and overstimulates the limbic system, which controls our behaviour, emotions, sex drive and survival instincts. Quite often, one feels hyperactive and overstimulated. Coffee triggers a fight-or-flight response in our body, which can last for several hours. And the withdrawal symptoms from coffee—headaches, mood swings and low energy—are equally difficult to manage.

If you are suffering from caffeine withdrawal symptoms, here is what you can do to heal.

1. Add one teaspoon of ghee sourced from a cruelty-free cow farm to your coffee. This helps protect your gut lining from the damage of caffeine.

2. Include herbs such as ashwagandha (Indian ginseng), chicory (blue dandelion), dandelion roots and brahmi (Indian pennywort) to make a warm drink. These herbs have adaptogenic and anti-inflammatory properties, which help release stress and reduce inflammation in the body. Ashwagandha translates to 'smell of the horse' and gives you the same energy boost as coffee does without the side-effects.

3. Add cinnamon, cardamom, clove, grated ginger, pepper and star anise to your coffee. Reduce the amount of coffee powder you use when preparing your cup, and consciously start cutting down on the amount of coffee you drink.

Most importantly, never drink coffee on an empty stomach, as it can rupture your sensitive stomach walls; and avoid coffee in the evenings, as it interferes with the production of melatonin and your sleep cycles. Again, many habitual coffee drinkers may not see symptoms as their bodies have started to suppress these messages, but the damage continues.

Addiction to any substance, be it coffee, sugar, alcohol or drugs, is harmful to your mental health too. Have you ever seen a little hamster going round and round on a Ferris wheel? That is what addictions and negative vices do to our bodies, minds and emotions. It destroys our personal and professional lives, relationships and marriages, because:

Addiction keeps pulling you back in, refusing to let you go.

These substances are not a replacement for love, and you cannot use them to fill up a void inside or simply numb your emotions. That's hardly the solution.

These are the three things you can do to break free from addiction: 1) Toughen up. Stop being soft on yourself and get ready to face your inner demons. Follow a military regimen with a fixed time to wake up, exercise and eat, and start cutting back by having one less cup of coffee, one less cigarette and one less glass of alcohol. Discipline is the only way out. 2) Seek help. The Ayurvedic panchakarma treatment helps in detoxifying the body from physical toxins, as well as remove the memories of those toxins so that you don't have a relapse. 3) And most importantly:

Fill yourself up with so much knowledge and light,
that the devil has no place to hide.

Once, a young girl travelled to our clinic from a different city, seeking a cure for her migraines. During our conversation, I asked her what was bothering her. She confessed that as they lived in a small factory town where there was nothing else to do, her husband and in-laws drank a lot of alcohol to the point of becoming addicted. Her marriage was hanging by a thin thread. After her migraines were treated, she told her sister-in-law and husband about us. They visited us too, and after intense detoxification, they never touched alcohol again. A few months later, I received a message from her stating that she wished to gift Prana herbal teas to everyone at her baby shower. Through sheer effort, she had fixed her health, helped her husband and family beat alcoholism, fixed her marriage and brought into this world a happy and healthy baby.

Every time you reach out to junk food or any addiction, ask yourself this critical question:

Am I feeding my disease or am I feeding my health?

This simple psychological trick will help you cut back on your addictions to unhealthy foods and get back on track to good health.

Dangerous health trends

It's crucial to stay away from diet trends that yield short-term gains but cause long-term damage. We have treated several patients in the clinic whose digestive systems were completely impaired after months of extreme dieting.

Crash dieting

It has the word 'crash' in it for a reason. In the initial days, you may see good results, but in the long run, your bones, muscles and tissues may become emaciated. And when you stop the diet, you often end up gaining all the weight you'd lost. If it took you six months to gain weight, give your body at least three months of disciplined exercise and dietary changes to get back in shape and stay in good health. Extremes like a no-carb diet can be fatal, as your brain literally runs on carbohydrates. And fat is your body's defence mechanism against deficiencies as it hoards up reserves, expecting a future health crisis. Make healthy choices.

Oil-free diet

Good fats, like those in cold-pressed oils, help lubricate the GI tract and allow the smooth movement of food and waste.

They are a rich source of bioflavonoids, oleic acid, omega 3 and omega 6 fatty acids, zinc, potassium, vitamins A, C, E and D and lecithin. Cold-pressed oils help boost the immune system, repair cellular damage in the body and reverse the ageing process. A complete fat-free or oil-free diet can cause excessive dryness in the system and trigger vata-related symptoms such as indigestion, chronic constipation, bone-related disorders because of a lack of lubricants in the body, and even chronic aches, fatigue, pain, anxiety, stress and symptoms of depression. Include good fats in your diet in the form of avocados, olives, coconut and cold-pressed oils.

Salt-free diet

The energetics of salt, as per Ayurveda, are fire and water. They stimulate digestion, metabolism, saliva and aid in absorbing nutrients from the food. Salt is laxative and emetic and helps lubricate your joints, muscles and nerves by holding moisture in your body. It has a calming effect when consumed in the right quantities. But when it is in excess, it can lead to water retention in the body. You can go on a salt-free diet for a day every week to help release water retention from the foods you have eaten. But completely cutting out salt can impair digestion.

Paleo diet

We don't live in caves anymore, so by that logic, we shouldn't be eating like cave-people. We don't have the same active lifestyle or live in the jungles like our earliest ancestors or cave-people did. Human beings have evolved and so has our digestive system since the stone age.

Keto diet

Initially, this high-fat, low-carb diet was designed to support those who have an autoimmune condition, wherein you feed the body fat to trick it into burning its fat reserves. However, if you don't have an autoimmune condition, following an extreme diet like this is going to break what your body was originally capable of.

Instead of these diets, simply follow a healthy lifestyle, remove all trigger foods and unhealthy junk, and personalize your diet plan based on your unique biological blueprint.

8

The Importance of Understanding the Digestion Period of Foods

In the food pyramid, fruits are considered the easiest to digest as they contain active microbial enzymes. They ideally require one hour in the stomach for digestion, one hour in the small intestines for assimilation of nutrients and one hour in the large intestine for absorption of moisture. Within three hours, they are ready for elimination and accumulate in the colon. Which is why, when we eat fruits, we usually get hungry after an hour or two, as the fruit is already digested and has moved from the stomach to the intestines.

Vegetables take a little longer to digest. They require two hours in the stomach for digestion, two hours in the small intestine for the assimilation of nutrients and two hours in the large intestine for absorption of moisture. In six hours, the body has collected unwanted waste in the colon and prepared for elimination. Which is why, when we have just a salad for lunch without any grains or cheese, we get hungry quickly after.

Of course, you may not have a bowel movement within three hours of eating fruits or six hours of eating a salad, as there may not be enough waste from these foods for the colon to release.

Grains, pulses, legumes, lentils, seeds and nuts have a longer shelf life and hence take longer to digest. They have a complex layer, which allows them to survive on the shelves naturally for over a year or more. They usually require six hours in the stomach for digestion, six hours in the small intestine for assimilation of nutrients and six hours in the large intestine for absorption of moisture. They require a total of eighteen hours in the gut to be fully digested, assimilated and absorbed before they are ready for elimination.

Monks, sages and several health gurus have trained their bodies to eat only one solid meal per day, which allows their bodies adequate rest and time to fully digest and absorb the nutrients. The one meal comprises lentils, vegetables and grains mixed together to make a filling porridge that satiates the body's need for carbohydrates, proteins and fibre. Yoga describes individuals based on the number of meals they consume. One who eats three meals a day is a *Rogi*, which means prone to diseases due to improper digestion. One who eats two meals a day is a *Bhogi*, which means someone who relishes food. One who eats one meal a day is a *Yogi*, one who is on the path of good health and spirituality. With practice and discipline, you can eliminate snacking between meals and reduce the number of meals you consume per day. By having one large meal or two meals a day, you are training your body to better absorb and assimilate the nutrients from these foods, and you will be able to give your digestive system adequate rest. When your digestive system is in a resting phase, your body actively utilizes and burns its fat reserves for energy.

Meat, seafood and eggs require the longest time in our system. They usually require twenty-four hours in the stomach for digestion, twenty-four hours in the small intestines for assimilation of nutrients and twenty-four hours in the large intestine for absorption of moisture. They spend over seventy-two hours in our system before they are ready for elimination. Imagine that instead of one piece of meat that occupies space in your gut for seventy-two hours, we could easily give our body nine to ten times more fruits and vegetables, which are a powerhouse of nutrients, vitamins, minerals and life-giving prana.

When you choose to heal, choose to heal all parts of your body, starting with kindness to your gut. This is the order of eating foods.

1. Always start with foods that take less time to digest, so start your day with fluids first to lubricate and cleanse your system. Follow with fruit or vegetable juices based on your body type. I will share some recipes in the next chapter.

2. Next, have some raw or stewed fruits, based on your digestive health, so they can enhance your gut flora. You can also have pre-soaked dry fruits along with your raw fruits in the morning to pack your day with essential nutrients, vitamins and minerals.

3. After an hour, you can have breakfast—for example, a simple porridge made from whole grains.

4. For lunch, you can have steamed salads, followed by a meal made of carbohydrates, proteins and vegetables, and follow this with a probiotic drink to enhance digestion.

5. For dinner, choose well-cooked and easy-to-digest foods like warm vegetable soups, steamed salads and porridge made from whole grains, millet, rice and lentils.

Avoid, or at least limit, the consumption of meat, seafood and eggs. As we age, and with experience, we naturally choose simpler foods for our gut as they enhance the quality of our lives.

Raw vs stewed fruits

If you have a healthy or normal digestive system, you can consume raw fruits and even raw vegetables to a certain extent, like carrots and cucumber. But if you have an impaired digestive system, raw foods can cause bloating, indigestion, and gas quite easily. In this case, you can stew the fruits with some water and warm spices, like cinnamon, clove, cardamom, and black pepper, to help cure constipation and indigestion symptoms. When you introduce cooked foods to your system, they are pre-digested, which accelerates the absorption and assimilation of nutrients.

Raw vs cooked vegetables

Many green vegetables, like spinach, chard, kale and bok choy, should not be juiced or consumed raw. Spinach and kale are powerhouses of nutrients, loaded with folic acid, minerals like iron, dietary fibre, and vitamins A, C and K. But they're also high in oxalic acid, which binds with calcium in your body, leading to kidney stones and interfering with the absorption and assimilation of nutrients. If anything, uncooked leafy greens irritate the gut lining and can cause irritable bowel syndrome, H. pylori, and small intestinal bacterial overgrowth (SIBO) in the long run.

Leafy green vegetables also often contain bacteria and even insecticides and pesticides on the surface, which can be toxic for our bodies. Of course, we wash our vegetables well, but any remaining bacteria may enter the gut, react with the anaerobic bacteria, and start releasing CO_2, methane and other gases, causing bloating, flatulence, and indigestion. Also, the fact is that our bodies cannot fully absorb nutrients from leafy green vegetables unless they are cooked.

Cruciferous vegetables, like cabbage, cauliflower and broccoli, are also difficult to digest in their raw form. They have high levels of oxalate that can impair your thyroid gland and kidney functions and cause severe bloating when consumed raw or in juice form.

Compare your digestive system to that of a herbivore, like a cow, whose main diet comprises leafy greens. Cows have two stomachs that aid in the digestion of leafy greens, but we have only one stomach compartment. Cows have 40,000 jaw movements per day. They chew their cud forty-five to sixty times per minute, return it to the rumen and bring it back at night to chew it all over again. Cows spend close to eight hours per day chewing their food. How many hours a day do we spend chewing our food? That's why humans evolved differently. We are the only social animals that went through a civilization process; we discovered fire, grew our food and cooked it to aid digestion.

There is a debate over whether plants feel pain. While some biologists say that plants don't have a brain and a nervous system and hence cannot perceive complex pain, other biologists claim that plants are social beings; they hold memories, nurse their sick members, respond to stimuli, perceive positive and negative energy, and have sensations that help them react to threats and survive. The smell of freshly cut grass is actually a chemical signal that plants release to signal to other plants about the presence of a predator, herbivore or land mower. Here is something interesting I found in Jain text.

The amount of pain living beings feel is directly proportionate to the number of senses and vitalities they have. The perception and gravity of pain increase with an increased number of senses and vitalities. There are two kinds of transmigrating souls: those with and without minds. *Amanaskas* are beings that are not capable of reasoning, for example, bacteria, plants, shells, ants, scorpions, etc. Their choices are driven by the functionality of their 'species' nature'. They are further divided into five categories based on the number of senses and vitalities they have.

One-sense organisms have four vitalities based on the physical body: the sense of touch, the strength of body or energy, respiration and life duration. They include plants, bacteria, and microorganisms living in the five elements of earth, water, fire, air and space. They take the physical form of the elements as their body form too.

Two-sense organisms have six vitalities, and they have a physical body and a mouth. They have the above four vitalities, a sense of taste and an organ of speech.

Three-sense organisms have seven vitalities. They have the above vitalities and a nose organ, which gives them a sense of smell. They include species like ants, bugs and insects.

Four-sense organisms have eight vitalities, which include the above vitalities and eyes, which give them sight. They include scorpions, spiders, bees, fish and other animals.

Five-sense organisms (without the mind) have nine vitalities, including all of the above and the sense of hearing. For instance, water snakes.

Five-sense organisms (with minds) are called *samanaskas*. They are beings who are capable of reasoning and include human beings and animals. They are capable of feeling complex emotions and emoting; they also have the gift of choice and can make complex emotional choices. They can choose their habitat, diet and relationships and fiercely protect their kith and kin. They have ten vitalities, which include four vitalities of the physical body (sense of touch, strength of body or energy, respiration and life duration), two vitalities of the mouth (sense of taste and organ of speech), sense of smell, sight, hearing and the tenth vitality, the mind.

The amount of pain a being experiences is directly proportionate to the number of sense organs they have that allows them to perceive pain. So by that theory, plants can experience emotions and pain, although simpler, whereas five, four, three and two-sense animals experience the complex amount of emotions and pain, directly proportionate to the number of senses that allows them to perceive the pain. This is another incentive to choose wisely what you put on your plate. The idea is to avoid or minimise violence on your plate, in your mind, thoughts, words and actions. Start with avoiding any violence towards the higher sense organisms, and once you have come to a minimal plant-based diet—eat steamed or cooked foods vs raw, and consume boiled water.

Another reason to cook, steam, boil or blanch all foods is to prevent them from releasing gases inside our bodies, to prevent diseases from the parasites found in raw foods, and to promote longevity. In fact, at our clinic, we have dealt with several patients who developed SIBO, H. pylori, anxiety and even clinical depression after going on a raw food diet for over a year.

Thus, make sure to blanch, steam, boil or cook all your leafy greens with mild spices and salt. You can blanch your spinach and kale in hot water for a few minutes, wash it off well and make a curry or paste out of it for your other dishes. Or you can make soup out of it. When you cook vegetables, you are breaking down the complex molecular pattern in plants, thus aiding easy absorption and assimilation of nutrients.

Now, the argument is that if I cook my food, I lose some nutrients. However, it's better to lose a small amount of nutrients than not be able to digest the food at all. Because:

If you can't digest the food, it is of no use to your system!

Grains vs the bloat

Grains, like legumes, lentils, nuts and seeds, have a thick outer layer and phytic acids, which give them a naturally long shelf life. So, ensure that you pre-soak all your grains, legumes, lentils, nuts and seeds overnight, or at least for four hours, before you cook them well. Softer grains like rice and seeds can be soaked for an hour, whereas harder-to-digest beans, nuts, legumes and lentils can be soaked overnight. For cancer patients, we in fact recommend soaking lentils for twenty-four hours and replacing the water it is soaked in every few hours to prevent fermentation. Soaking helps soften the outer layer and phytic acids, which are not easy for our body to break down or digest.

Make sure to also add vegetables to your grains, as they are loaded with fibre that helps move food in the gut. Remember, the food has to journey through almost twenty-eight feet of small and large intestines!

Add some warm spices such as cinnamon, cardamom, clove, grated ginger, black peppercorns and star anise to stimulate the metabolic fire in the food and your system. You can also add some carminative spices like cumin, fennel, coriander and carom seeds, which help stimulate the digestive juices and also prevent the growth of parasites in the intestines.

Fasting

The digestive organs are the largest in the body and they require a tremendous amount of energy and rest. It includes the oesophagus, stomach, duodenum, small and large intestines, and colon. The organs that support the digestive system include the liver, gall bladder, pancreas and biliary tree. The liver is, in fact, the largest detoxifying organ in our body, which purifies blood day in and day out. Resting the digestive tract frees up a huge amount of energy, which can be used for repairing muscles, tissues, organs, skin, hair and other tissues. The new energy is also used to improve agni, clear unwanted toxins, and support a strong immune system. With fasting, the digestive organs get a complete break and can now focus on detoxification. The body becomes lighter and regains its natural strength.

Fasting helps in using up all the stored fats, glucose and ketones in your body, which helps in fighting inflammation, heart-related disorders, triglycerides, cholesterol and all kinds of lifestyle diseases and even insulin resistance. There is proven research[*] that shows fasting for up to seventy-two hours can completely regenerate your immune system because it helps break down the white blood cells in large numbers and signals the body to generate a new immune system. Fasting helps improve brain function and prevent neurodegenerative disorders. Your mind becomes clearer and your awareness, consciousness and ability to focus and generate new ideas are also heightened when your digestive system is at rest. Your gut–brain axis strengthens, your intuition improves and, thus, your ability to make better decisions becomes easier. This is why many spiritual traditions use fasting to increase spiritual growth and openness. Just as we use meditation to clear our minds, fasting helps clean our digestive system.

Learning how to fast is an important part of understanding how to take care of our bodies and minds. Engage in fruit fasting, salt-free fasting, water fasting or dry fasting at least once a week. I usually ask my patients to fast on Mondays, as it helps release

---

[*] Matt Van Sol, 'Fasting for 72 Hours Can Reset Your Entire Immune system', The Source, November 21, 2018, https://thesource.com/2018/11/21/fasting-for-72-hours-can-reset-your-entire-immune-system/, accessed on June 8, 2023.

toxins, gases, bloat, undigested foods and water retention from the excess salt, oil and junk foods consumed over the weekend.

You can consume fruits in raw form or juice form all day and break your fast by sunset with a bowl of well-cooked grains, pulses and vegetables, or tapioca, which is a good source of carbohydrates and starch. Do not wait until late in the night to break your fast, as it defeats the purpose. Fruit fasting allows the body to better absorb important nutrients, vitamins and minerals from these easy-to-digest food groups. You can eventually improve your capacity to fast for twenty-four hours and do water fasting for one to three days at a time. When you give your body and digestive system adequate rest, your body heals itself.

9

Food Chemistry

Food chemistry is called *viruda ahar* in Ayurveda. It is a unique concept that talks about food-to-food interactions and food-processing interactions. Any food that is the wrong combination, has been processed incorrectly, is consumed in an incorrect dosage or at the wrong time of the day or season can have a toxic effect on your body. They lead to an accumulation of what is called *ama* in Ayurveda, or poison.

It can trigger diseases, particularly of the skin.

January 2020. Just before the world was hit by chaos, my world took a turn for the worse. I attended a women's festival conducted in an ashram in a remote town in Rajasthan. Women flew in from all over the world. We had about 200 participants from over fifty countries. The winter in Rajasthan, which is a desert region, is usually very harsh. The weather was dry; the sun was strong and the cold was severe at night. I am a pitta (fire) dominant body type with sensitive skin that reacts quickly to heat. I had the foods served in the ashram without paying much regard to the combinations on my plate. There were fruits, vegetables and grains all served in one go to save time. I had the local chillies in all my meals. My skin started to itch and burn, and I ignored it for some time. Then I started applying the local ghee to ease the burning. But by the end of the festival, my skin had developed a severe allergic and inflammatory reaction to the food, triggering a skin disorder called urticaria. It is a painful rash that spreads all over the body, along with swelling, burning sensations and continuous itching. And it is always triggered by an allergic reaction to specific foods.

On the flight back home, I dipped a tissue in water and placed it on my face to ease the burning sensation. But the heat from my skin was so severe that the tissue dried up in a fraction of a second and got glued to my skin in fragments. I was in tears. I couldn't blink, move my facial muscles or even speak without experiencing excruciating pain. And when I sneezed, my nose would start bleeding uncontrollably. By the time I reached home, my face, chest and arms were covered with burnt inflamed skin. It felt like it was on fire, even though I had no fever. My face dried up like an autumn leaf, and I carried a flask of ice with me to ease the burning so I could just breathe. I was shaken. I thought I would never be able to face my clients or the camera again.

I was lucky that I had already set up Prana. My in-house doctors examined me and said it was so severe that it could take anywhere between six and twelve months for me to recover fully. I had no choice but to wait and watch. I have unconditional faith in Ayurveda and started an intense detoxification (panchakarma) treatment under their guidance. I spent two to four hours per day in the treatment room, where my therapists carefully massaged medicated herbal ghee into my burnt skin to release the toxins. I underwent abhyangam, which is a full-body medicated massage, along with takradhara, which is the pouring of medicated buttermilk on the forehead, to reduce the metabolic fire. This was combined with intense herbal enema sessions to release the poison from my body, a simple mono diet of only khichdi for days, and strong Ayurvedic medication. I also met with Dr Aparna, an allopath and skin specialist, who refused to put me on steroid injections or oral steroids, as most doctors would have with the gravity of the situation. She said that I was showing remarkable progress and asked me to go through the ayurvedic cleanse and gave me steroid-based creams and basic medicines to use in case I couldn't bear the pain.

Within two weeks, much to the pleasant surprise of my doctors and therapists, my burnt skin started falling off, albeit in a thick, crystal-like form. This was the degree of damage done to my skin. But soon I had brand-new skin that looked visibly younger, softer, plumper and healthier than ever before in my life. My doctors said this early recovery was also due to the placebo effect—a strong mental and emotional desire to recover—which allowed the medication to show such quick results at a physical level. Remember, the body has a 1:1 relationship, and the body simply mirrors at a cellular level what we emote at a mental and emotional level. From that day onwards, my skin has always been a map that I read to gauge my gut and internal health, and I never take my health or my diet for granted.

Forbidden food combinations

Fruits with other foods

The biggest mistake you are making with your fruits is mixing them with other food groups. It is the leading cause of skin disorders such as psoriasis, eczema, rosacea and urticaria. Most fruits contain active acids like malic acid, tartaric acid, folic acid, oxalic acid, ascorbic acid, citric acid and active microbial enzymes, some fruits like melons contain complex acids like tetrdecanoic acid, pentadecanoic acid, hexadecanoic acid, heptadecanoic acid, octadecanoic acid and eicosanoic acid which aid the digestion process. But these fruit acids react quickly with the acids and enzymes found in other food groups. These are the combinations that you must definitely avoid.

Fruits and dairy

One of the deadliest combinations is fruits mixed with dairy products like milk, yoghurt and cheese. Dairy products contain lactic acid, which reacts with fruit acids, leading to a chemical reaction inside our gut that damages the gut lining and causes leaky gut syndrome. It can lead to this toxic by-product entering our bloodstream, where it can get deposited in various organs, especially under the skin. Specifically, the following are certain ways fruits react with dairy:

Citric fruits and dairy. When citric fruits like lemon, tomato, tamarind, oranges and pineapples are mixed with dairy (milk, yoghurt or cheese), they cause the milk to coagulate, which can lead to gastric issues and heartburn. These fruits are acidic in nature and are a rich source of vitamin C, which reacts with the lactic acid found in milk. That is why pasta sauce with tomatoes and dairy-based cream or cheese, gives discomfort to many, especially those who are pitta (fire) dominant.

Fruit with dairy has an instant ill effect on infants and young kids. Once, I noticed my therapist giving her breastfeeding toddler a bowl of grapes to eat. I immediately took the grapes away, but I wasn't sure how much she had already had. The next day, the therapist told us that the little one had cried all night from a severe tummy ache and painful cramps. We had to wait for her first bowel movement for the toxic by-product to be released.

Melons and dairy. Milk is laxative in nature and melons are diuretic; therefore, it causes a clash of actions in your stomach and can lead to severe indigestion, IBS and chronic diarrhoea symptoms. The stomach acids required to digest the melons will cause the milk to curdle and cause gastric issues. Your body produces different digestive enzymes based on the kind of foods you have consumed, so it's best to eat melons separately and not mix them with other fruits either. Melons contain bio-active compounds such as carotenoids, amino acids, vanillic acids, ascorbic acids and trans-cinnamic acids, which react with the lactic acid found in milk. In fact, melons react sharply with other fruit groups also and can cause indigestion, IBS, reflux and other symptoms. Its best to eat melons separately with an hour's gap from other meals.

Sweet fruits with dairy. Apples and bananas too do not mix well with milk. Bananas and milk are a very heavy combination to digest, which can cause fatigue and sluggishness in the body while you are trying to digest it. But if you must have a banana milkshake, add a pinch of cinnamon or nutmeg powder to promote digestion. It is best to avoid giving children banana milkshakes, as they aggravate kapha symptoms such as mucus build-up, colds, coughs, sinusitis, asthma, hay fever and allergies. Apples and milk are also an unhealthy combination. Apples contain active enzymes, malic acid and citric acid, which react with the lactic acid found in milk, and they also start to oxidize on exposure and turn black. You do not want to put this combination in your tummy.

It is always better to chew fruit and drink the milk separately after an hour's gap.

Fruits with vegetables, grains, pulses and meat

As mentioned earlier, fruits require only one hour in the stomach for digestion, one hour in the small intestine for absorption and assimilation of nutrients, and one hour in the large intestine. But vegetables require twice the amount of time, and grains require three times the amount of time to be fully digested, absorbed and assimilated in our stomach, small intestine and large intestine. So, when we mix fruits with complex food groups like vegetables and grains, it stresses the digestive system. Often, the undigested vegetables and grains keep the fruit longer than needed in the stomach, causing the fruit acids to react with the stomach acids. This can trigger reflux, burning sensations and even ulcers in the long run. Or, when you eat fruit after a heavy meal, the easily digested fruit pushes the undigested vegetables and grains into the small intestine, causing bloating and fermentation of the undigested foods and thus gases.

When fruits are cooked or stewed, the acid property changes and they react less with grains. For example, baked apple pie or orange cake is consumed as a dessert in some parts of the world, and your body can withstand it because you consume them in small potions once in a blue moon. But, if you consume them regularly, you will start experiencing signs of unease. Like raw or stewed fruits mixed with oats, has become a go-to breakfast bowl for many. Although it looks healthy, the heavier nature of the cereal grain and the light nature of the fruit will make the digestive system sluggish in the long run, causing fatigue and loss of energy. And if this bowl contains milk, it will cause symptoms of IBS and diarrhoea where the body attempts to push out the toxic by-product of dairy and fruit instantly.

Fruits with nightshades

Fruits like cucumber and melons react with nightshades such as tomatoes, potatoes, eggplant, peppers, goji berries and cherries, as they have conflicting properties. Nightshades contain alkaloids that react quickly with the malic acid found in cucumbers, and the fruit acids found in melons. Even though the tomato is botanically a fruit, it is considered a vegetable in the culinary world, as it's best digested in its cooked form. Alkaloids found in tomatoes can impact the gut lining when consumed excessively in their raw form.

Cucumber with lemon. Cucumber is a rich source of cucurbitin, which is a mild anti-diuretic, whereas lemon is citric and diuretic. These are opposite qualities that can clash in the stomach and cause indigestion and burping.

Fruits with meat

This is considered a poisonous combination and is a strict no-no. Meat takes over seventy-two hours to get fully digested by the body, and the presence of easy-to-digest fruits will cause indigestion and severe gut issues in the long run.

The golden rule is:

Eat fruit alone or leave it alone.

You can have fruits either raw, stewed or in juice form. But eat fruits by themselves as a separate meal. Ensure that you keep a two-hour gap after a solid meal before eating fruit. And if you have eaten fruit, wait an hour before eating other foods.

Even within fruits, it's best not to mix them together. Fruits are categorized into three different groups based on the actions they perform in the body, which we will discuss in the next chapter.

One of the worst health trends is smoothies. Smoothies look appealing in a social media picture but are terrible for your gut when made without regard to the food's chemistry. We will talk about this in detail in the next chapter. In fact, some of these combinations can cause instant poisoning in an infant and trigger severe health issues such as coeliac disease, vomiting, diarrhoea, tummy aches, leaky gut syndrome and discomfort.

I have often met mothers who come to me with infants suffering from serious gut health issues. This is due to the wrong combination of foods the mother was eating, and the presence of sour foods like lemons, tomatoes, tamarind and tangerines that caused the mother's breast milk to break in the infant's tummy.

Safe fruit combinations

Fruits with nuts. Fruits can be mixed with nuts and dried fruits, as they come from the same food group. However, nuts take longer to chew and even digest. So, make sure to pre-soak your nuts overnight before garnishing your fruit salads with them. Soaking nuts also removes the phytic acid found in them which is associated with indigestion; and it enables the body to better absorb nutrients like iron, zinc, calcium and protein found in them.

Fruits with plant-based milk. Fruits can also be mixed with plant-based milk, as they come from the same food group and do not react with each other.

Mango with milk. The mango is called 'the king of all fruits', as it's loaded with several essential nutrients and vitamins. Mangoes have a heaty effect on the body, whereas milk has a cooling effect on the tummy. When combined together, mangoes and milk cancel the heat and keep the digestive fire in balance. For this smoothie, ensure you use only ripe and sweetened mangoes where the fruit acids have mellowed with age. Avoid mixing raw or sour mangoes with milk, as they have a high concentration of fruit acids, which can cause the milk to break.

Avocado with milk. This is a safe combination, as the avocado doesn't react with the lactic acid and helps promote weight gain.

Garlic with milk. This may sound strange, but garlic has anti-inflammatory and pain-relieving properties. In Ayurvedic home remedies, a pod of garlic is boiled in milk and given to a patient to relieve joint aches. However, do not try this at home without first consulting with an Ayurvedic doctor as the combination may make you nauseous if you are sensitive to strong smells.

In order to aid the digestion of fruits, you can add some condiments. For example, muskmelon has complex water in it that can lead to burping for some people. It has a diuretic property, is a mild laxative, contains glutamic acid, alanine and aspartic acid in larger quantities and arginine, glycine, lysine and proline in smaller quantities. To aid digestion and prevent burping or bloating from muskmelon, you can sprinkle some organic, unrefined sugar on it to sweeten it and release the gases.

Similarly, watermelon is also diuretic. It contains five unsaturated fatty acids (9-hexadecenoic acid, 9-octadecenoic acid, 9,12-octadecadienoic acid [Z,Z], 8, 11-octadecadienoic acid and 9,12,15-octadecatrienoic acid). To aid easy digestion, sprinkle a pinch of black pepper and pink salt. This prevents dehydration after consuming melons.

Pomegranate has citric, malic, oxalic and tartaric acids. For some people who have a sensitive throat, pomegranate juice can cause a sore throat, dryness and discomfort. You can add a pinch of black pepper and pink salt to prevent the drying effect of pomegranate and aid digestion.

Grapes can give children and kapha-dominant people a cold quite easily. Soak them in warm water for some time to reduce their kapha property and prevent colds and coughs.

Astringent fruits such as apples, berries, cherries, strawberries and blackberries will leave some with dry mouth syndrome and can cause mild dehydration and constipation in vata-dominant body types. You can stew these fruits and add warm spices such as cinnamon, clove, cardamom and pepper to aid digestion and cure constipation symptoms.

Sweet fruits like bananas, mangoes and avocados, which create more mucus in the body, are best consumed during the first half of the day. Avoid consuming any fruit after sunset, as it activates the body, delays melatonin production and affects the sleep cycle.

Forbidden dairy combinations

Milk with fruits. As discussed, this is a strictly forbidden combination as it can cause undigested metabolic waste due to the incompatibility of fruit and dairy acids. The acidic by-product impacts the gut lining often triggering leaky gut syndrome, which causes toxins to leak into the bloodstream and get deposited in various organs. The body in a desperation to get rid of the toxins sometimes rushes these to the surface of the skin hoping to release them through the pores in the form of sweat, but when the toxins are too large, they get deposited under the skin causing chronic skin disorders like psoriasis, eczema, urticaria and others. All dairy products like milk, yoghurt and cheese, are incompatible with fruits due to the presence of lactic acid, which reacts with fruit acids.

Milk with vegetables. Vegetables, especially radish, which is very heaty, react sharply to dairy products. It causes the heat to go up in your stomach and slow down the digestion process. Milk is incompatible with nightshade vegetables such as tomatoes, potatoes, peppers and brinjal, and even other vegetables like bitter gourd and lady finger, as they can trigger infections, eczema and indigestion. Lady finger has essential amino acids like tryptophan and lysine and has a sticky glue-like property that can react with milk and block the digestive passages. Bitter gourd and milk, if consumed within the same hour, can trigger constipation, pain and a burning sensation in the stomach. There are some preparations that are exceptions to this rule. Carrot is considered a neutral vegetable that doesn't react much with other food groups and can be cooked with sweetened milk and spices to make carrot halwa, a traditional recipe in India.

Milk with salty snacks. Often during the monsoons, some of us have the habit of having milk tea with a side of salty snacks and delicacies. But the salt in these delicacies causes the milk to curdle, which can impair your gut lining in the long run and even cause stomach cramps.

Milk with yoghurt. Never use milk with yoghurt as a dressing for your vegetables or salad because it causes blockages in your channels, which are called *strotas* in Ayurveda, and can lead to infections and tummy health issues. Milk and yoghurt are at different stages of the metabolic process and are two complex proteins that shouldn't be mixed together. Yoghurt is a fermented product that when mixed with milk, blocks the channels in our body, triggering stomach issues, infections, acidity, heartburn, diarrhoea and bloating.

Safe milk combinations

Milk can be safely mixed with warm spices such as turmeric for better immunity, a pinch of nutmeg to improve sleep quality and ghee to clear constipation symptoms. It can also be mixed with cinnamon, cardamom, clove, ginger powder and star anise to improve immunity and with dried nuts to build stamina. Dried nuts and dry fruits are almost as low in sugar as vegetables and contain very little or negligible amounts of fruit enzymes and citric acid, thus making them a safe, non-reactive combination.

Forbidden yoghurt combinations

Yoghurt with fruits. Again, fruits have active microbial enzymes and fruit acids, which react sharply with the bacteria in yoghurt and curd. The heat causes further fermentation of the fruits with the yoghurt, leading to severe blockages of your body's channels and even skin issues. Even mangoes must not be mixed with yoghurt, as both are heaty in nature. Do not add grapes, bananas, apples, berries or any fruit flavours to your yoghurt. Although FMCG companies have flooded the market with flavoured yoghurts and called them healthy, this is the leading cause of the accumulation of ama, or poison, in our bodies and under the skin.

Yoghurt with nightshade vegetables. Do not mix yoghurt or curd with vegetables like tomatoes, potatoes, eggplant and peppers, as it can lead to indigestion and bloating. Yoghurt has active bacterial enzymes and lactic acid, which reacts with the alkaloids and citric acids found in nightshades. Yoghurt with radish especially can cause severe pain and indigestion symptoms. Also, never add sour foods like lemon, tamarind paste, to yoghurt or curd as it causes them to curdle and break in your stomach leading to gases and even reflux.

Yoghurt with cheese. This combination is also forbidden in Ayurveda, as the chemical reaction between yoghurt and cheese which are at two different stages of the metabolic process, impairs the digestive system.

Yoghurt with legumes (lentils, pulses, seeds, peas). This combination can lead to gases, bloating, indigestion and even diarrhoea.

Safe yoghurt combinations

The only vegetables and fruits that can be safely added to yoghurt as condiments are grated carrot, beetroot and cucumber.

You should also never consume plain yoghurt or curd. Remember to always add cumin powder, pink salt, cilantro, chillies or tempered mustard seeds to aid the digestion process and prevent the accumulation of mucus in the body. Although there is a debate on adding salt as it kills the good bacteria in the curd and yoghurt, a small amount of salt aids digestion and prevents further fermentation of the yoghurt in our gut. It's the same principle as followed with salted *chaas*, which is yoghurt or curd diluted with water, and with added condiments like pink salt, cumin, cilantro, chilly, curry leaf and even a pinch of asafoetida to aid digestion. This diluted drink is in fact considered tri-doshic in nature which means it is suitable for all body types and almost all seasons.

Alternately, you can also have sweetened yoghurt by adding honey to it, which has a calming effect on the nervous system and helps reduce anxiety or nervousness. Definitely avoid consuming yoghurt or curd post-sunset, as it leads to the accumulation of mucus and susceptibility to colds, coughs, sinusitis and weight gain issues.

Forbidden cheese combinations

Cheese with milk, yoghurt, fruit, beans, hot drinks or eggs. Milk, cheese and yoghurt are at different stages of metabolic food processing and should never be clubbed together. Cheese is a fermented dairy product that has cultures of lactic acid, bacterial enzymes, and complex proteins that quickly react with most food groups, causing gas, delays in digestion and gut issues. Cheese is, however, paired with wine in many countries, as it prevents the wine from burning the digestive system, and the wine helps prevent cheese from getting stuck to the gut lining. Again, this combination is consumed in moderation, excess of which can impair the gut walls.

Forbidden grain combinations

Grains with fruits. Avoid mixing grains with fruits, as the time required to digest fruits is just three hours, whereas grains require eighteen hours. The combination can lead to undigested grains getting pushed into the small intestine, triggering indigestion, fermentation of foods, bloating and gas.

Grains and tapioca. Tapioca is a rich source of starch and, when mixed with other grains, can trigger symptoms of stomach pain, bloating, gas and nausea.

Grains are best cooked with some amount of water, spices, ghee and vegetables to aid digestion and the easy absorption of nutrients. Make sure to pre-soak your grains for a few hours and cook them well in order to dissolve the phytic acids. The fibre in the vegetables aids the downward movement of grains, and you can even add a pinch of asafoetida, grated ginger, garlic, carrom seeds, cumin seeds, bay leaf, and other warm spices to prevent indigestion from grains.

Forbidden protein combinations

Proteins with other proteins. Mixing any two different proteins— milk, yoghurt, dairy, cheese, lentils, eggs or tofu—causes stress on the digestive system, especially on the liver and kidneys. Consume one type of protein at a time. Beans, especially when mixed with dairy or animal-based products, can cause immediate discomfort in the stomach, like bloating and gas. Ensure you consume lentils, beans and yoghurt separately to aid in the complete absorption of the nutrients.

Protein with starch and fats. When mixed, this combination causes delays in digestion and absorption. Protein is best cooked with some water, warm spices and vegetables to aid digestion.

Remember to avoid these combinations of foods the next time you sit down to have a snack or a meal. If you are ever confused about the combination of foods to have and which ones to avoid, simply mix any fruit with dairy or one food group with other food groups and leave it out for some time. After an hour, check for any discolouration in the food or a rancid smell. This is a sign that these food groups react negatively to each other and are unsuitable for consumption.

Deep-fried potato chips

Did you know that the deep frying of potatoes can develop toxic substances such as acrylamide, which can prove to be carcinogenic? Scientists have known for years[*] that acrylamide is capable of causing nerve damage in humans,[†][‡] including muscle weakness and impaired muscle coordination, particularly from industrial exposure to large levels of the chemical. In fact, any vegetable or carb-rich food, when deep fried, baked or grilled loses all its nutrients and releases toxic substances that impair the gut. Boiling and steaming vegetables is a healthier alternative and does not release acrylamide. You can also include healthy snacks like lotus seeds, lentil crackers, fruits and nuts. In Asian countries, there are delicacies like pakoras and samosas where vegetables are deep fried with an outer layer like gram flour, which acts as a barrier between the vegetable and the hot oil, thus preventing the chemical by-product of acrylamide. But remember to consume any deep-fried foods in moderation.

---

[*] Agency for Toxic Substances and Disease Registry, 'ToxFAQs™ for Acrylamide', Centres for Disease Control and Prevention, https://wwwn.cdc.gov/TSP/ToxFAQs/ToxFAQsDetails.aspx?faqid=1162&toxid=236#:~:text=The%20main%20targets%20of%20acrylamide,reported%20in%20some%20acrylamide%20workers, June 8, 2023.

[†] About Cancer, 'Acrylamide and Cancer Risk', National Cancer Institute (2017), https://www.cancer.gov/about-cancer/causes-prevention/risk/diet/acrylamide-fact-sheet, June 8, 2023.

[‡] Food, 'Acrylamide and Diet, Food Storage, and Food Preparation', U.S. Food and Drug Administration (2022), https://www.fda.gov/food/process-contaminants-food/acrylamide-and-diet-food-storage-and-food-preparation#:~:text=Comparing%20frying%2C%20roasting%2C%20and%20baking,potatoes%E2%80%9D%20does%20not%20produce%20acrylamide, June 8, 2023.

Never heat honey

Honey should never be cooked, warmed or heated because it turns toxic, leading to the accumulation of ama, which is poison in the digestive tract. When heated, the sugar and fructose in the honey change their chemical composition and increase the production of a toxic substance called 5-hydroxymethylfurfural (HMF). It is called a browning effect or the Maillard Reaction. Heated honey (>140°C) mixed with an equal quantity of ghee also produces HMF, which has a severe damaging effect on our health. Ayurveda states that the effects of heated honey are so severe on our bodies, that it may take years to reverse the damage. In India, a preparation called *panchamrit*, made from a combination of sugar, honey, curd, milk and ghee, is offered to the gods and consumed by devotees as *prasadam*. But these are consumed in very small quantities and not as a complete meal, which the digestive system can handle. Heated honey mixed with ghee also produces HMF which may cause deleterious effects. Mixing ghee and honey in an equal ratio can also turn toxic and can invite trouble for your health. On mixing ghee and honey, a substance called Clostridium botulinum spreads rapidly in the body and can lead to respiratory problems, stomach ache, and even cancer. Clostridium botulinum is a type of bacteria that can produce dangerous toxins, especially under low-oxygen conditions.

Honey can be mixed in warm milk or water up to 42°C or body temperature. Place your pinkie finger in your drink for five to ten seconds to check if the heat is bearable. Only then should you add honey.

Honey is medicine, not food!

It is not a sweetener for your hot beverages and should never be baked into your desserts. In fact, packaged cereals coated with honey are produced at very high temperatures, which are extremely unhealthy and slow poison. Do not consume honey if you have symptoms like hyperacidity, acid reflux, burning sensations or fever, as honey gets solidified due to elevated body temperatures, thus blocking the srotas—the channels and ducts in our body through which nutrients flow. Honey can be given to children over the age of one and to pregnant women. The best way to have honey is to mix 1 teaspoon of it with ½ teaspoon of grated ginger. You can also add a piece of pepper, turmeric and cinnamon and consume it raw on an empty stomach. This helps in releasing colds, coughs, bronchial disorders and lung congestion, and it also helps with weight loss by dissolving the mucus and sticky substances that block the passages in our body.

10

Improve Your Relationship with Food

Five habits to work on:

1. **Eat only when you're hungry.** Your body provides digestive juices and signals to you when it is ready for a new meal. Don't eat without an appetite; otherwise, the food sits in the gut for hours, leading to indigestion.
2. **Eat until you're 80 per cent full.** Your stomach is the size of your fist, so eat until you're 80 per cent full, and then there will be room for the digestive juices and stomach acids to work. Your stomach is like a blender; if you fill it up to the top, it will not be able to function. In fact, for a meal, yogis will eat 50 per cent solid foods, 25 per cent liquids, and leave room for digestive juices.
3. **Drink your solids and eat your liquids.** This means chewing your food until it turns into liquid. Chewing creates saliva, which aids in the digestion process. Do not make a smoothie of all your foods, as that eliminates the chewing process and stresses the stomach. Instead of

fruit juice, have raw fruits; instead of a smoothie, have warm, well-cooked soups with spices that stimulate the metabolic fire and aid the digestion process. Instead of junk, have home-cooked foods like porridge. To eat your liquids means to sit down while drinking water. Do not gulp on the go, as the water rushes to the lower belly and the body doesn't get time to absorb all the nutrients and minerals found in drinking water.

4. **Do not eat with electronic distractions.** Remember, the gut is communicating with the brain, so if you are distracted when you're eating—with a mobile phone or television—the brain struggles to focus on digestion, which can lead to bloating, overeating, acidity and indigestion.

5. **Engage your senses.** Use your fingers, taste buds, olfactory senses, eyes and ears to carry messages to the brain about the kind of food you are eating. The brain sends messages to the gut on what kind of digestive juices to make for the new guest.

Soup vs smoothie

The one common dish you will find in almost all food cultures around the world is soup. And the one thing you will not find in the cultural history of food in any part of this world, is smoothies. Smoothies are an invention of the West and a by-product of busy lives, wherein all the ingredients are blended together and consumed as a drink. It's a quick-fix solution with short-term results but long-term damage to the gut, colon and even your mental and emotional health.

Soups, on the other hand, nourish your body, mind and soul. You can make soup out of literally anything, including potatoes, carrots, beetroot, leeks, spinach, celery, moringa, spirulina and lentils. It's a nourishing bowl loaded with the nutrients, vitamins and minerals that your body needs. Add some simple carminative spices to it to stimulate agni and aid digestion, absorption and assimilation.

Human beings are the only species that have gone through the civilization process and can grow and cook their food. We must use this knowledge wisely for our greater good. In fact, the best discovery by humans has been fire, which is also called God in many religions and cultures. We also have within us a digestive fire called *jatharagni*, which is responsible for metabolizing food. This agni keeps our internal organs warm and keeps us alive. It is responsible for all digestive and transformative processes that help build new tissues from the foods we have eaten. Well-cooked, warm foods and soups help support this agni in our body and prevent cellular damage.

The worst human invention is the blender. We dump in all the wrong combinations of fruits, vegetables and dairy with complete disregard for food chemistry and make a drinkable meal, thinking we are doing our body a favour! On the contrary, smoothies diminish the agni and weaken the digestive system in the long run. And the wrong combinations of food groups further trigger a reaction because of the contradicting chemicals found in different foods, creating undigested metabolic waste and damaging the gut lining. Consuming the wrong combination of foods is the leading cause of symptoms of IBS, including bloating, indigestion, reflux, colon health issues, leaky gut syndrome and skin diseases. Nature has given us thirty-two teeth to chew our food. When you chew your food, it creates that much saliva that aids digestion in the stomach. Remember, digestion begins in the mouth, not the stomach.

Juicing

Juicing has many health benefits, such as cleansing and detoxifying the gut and improving the absorption of nutrients, leading to healthy skin and digestion. Juices are best consumed in the morning after 200 ml of warm water. You can also go on a juice fast for one day, three days or more, depending on your capacity. But as soon as your metabolic fire becomes active, ensure that you start eating soft, solid foods to prevent reflux symptoms.

Again, we need to be careful of the permutations and combinations of foods juiced together. Avoid juicing leafy green vegetables, as they are home to parasites that can enter the blood stream easily; spinach and kale are particularly linked to kidney stones when consumed without cooking. (See Chapter 9 for a detailed explanation of the wrong combination of foods.)

Fruits

You can juice all fruits but avoid mixing them. Have the juice of a single fruit at a time, as fruits have active acids in them, like citric acid, malic acid, oxalic acid, and fumaric acid, which react with each other, causing a burning sensation and rupturing the gut lining.

Fruits are of three different natures: astringent, sweet and sour. If you have to mix fruits, ensure they are from the same taste group. The exception would be melons, which must be eaten alone. Melons are a rich source of folate, vitamins B1, B3 and B6, fruit acids and diuretic properties. Do not mix melons with any other fruit group, as they quickly cause bloating and indigestion symptoms. So, watermelon and muskmelon should be eaten by themselves.

Astringent fruits have a drying property, which helps tighten the collagen and tissues. You can mix apples, pears, blackberries, blueberries, cherries, strawberries, blackthorn (sloe berries), dry figs, pomegranates, aronia chokeberries, chokecherries, bird cherries, quince, unripe persimmon, banana peels or unripe bananas West and cashew apples.

Sweet fruits help build new tissues and create mucus when consumed in excess. You can mix sweet fruits like mangoes, pomegranates, ripe bananas, amla, stewed apples and pears, fresh dates, custard apples, wood apples and grapes. Here, pomegranates can be both sweet and astringent, depending on how ripe the fruit is.

Sour fruits have a cleansing property and help lighten the tissues from within. Citric fruits like lemons, tangerines, oranges and grapefruit can be mixed, while fruits like sour grapes, plums, sour mangoes, kiwi, rhubarb, tart cherries, gooseberries and cranberries can be mixed together.

Botanically speaking, although cucumber, tomato, aubergine, zucchini and peppers are considered fruits because of the presence of seeds, they are treated as vegetables in the culinary world as they are easily compatible with other vegetable groups and need to be cooked.

Vegetables

Below are some of the best and safest vegetable juice combinations:

Ash gourd juice: If you are overweight or have symptoms of a cold or cough, sinusitis, abdominal distention, bloating, heaviness or a sluggish metabolism, then ash gourd is the perfect remedy for cleansing your digestive system and eliminating toxins accumulated in the gut. It acts like a rough sponge, cleansing the gut from the inside, and the bitterness in this vegetable causes your gut to release all waste and parasites. However, if you have symptoms of constipation, dry skin, dry hair and body aches and pains, which are vata imbalances, avoid this juice as it may aggravate the imbalance and the symptoms.

You can add a pinch of salt and black pepper to your green juices to prevent water retention or indigestion from the gases released by plants.

Celery and cucumber juice: Celery has been hailed as a magic vegetable for its anti-inflammatory properties. If you are experiencing symptoms of inflammation, swelling and water retention, the roughage and fibre from celery can help you cleanse your gut of toxins that are causing these symptoms. Cucumber is a natural diuretic and detox drink; it helps flush the toxins out and balances the bitter taste of celery.

Cilantro and cucumber juice: Cilantro juice helps reduce the risk of heart disease, diabetes, obesity and seizures, and also helps improve energy levels and the texture of your hair and skin. Cucumber helps balance this drink with its diuretic effect.

Carrot and beetroot juice: This powerhouse drink is loaded with vitamin C and antioxidants, has cytotoxin action and as well as anti-cancer benefits. Consuming this drink reduces cancer cell development, reduces blood pressure, improves the texture of skin and hair, reduces soreness and pain in muscles after workouts, and helps detoxify the system. Beetroot has betaine, which improves liver health functions, and nitrate, which improves blood circulation and oxygenation within the brain. It is an excellent drink for those suffering from PCOS, PCOD, infertility, low haemoglobin levels, thalassemia minor and those recuperating from chemotherapy.

Bitter gourd and tomato juice: Also known as balsam apple, balsam pear, bitter apple, lakwa, margose, wild cucumber or bitter cucumber, bitter gourd is an underrated but most-prized ingredient in your kitchen. Unfortunately, the vegetable is disliked by many due to its strong, bitter taste. Bitter gourd is loaded with vitamins C, B1, B2, B3 and B9, tannins, flavonoids, iron and magnesium. It contains twice the amount of potassium as bananas and twice the amount of calcium as spinach and broccoli. Add tomato to this juice, which is a powerhouse of vitamin C and helps balance the bitterness of the bitter gourd.

Banana stem juice: This is your secret to losing weight quickly! Juicing this takes a lot of effort, but trust me, it is worth it. My parents lost about 10 kg when they started consuming banana stem juice along with yoga. Banana stem juice is an excellent source of fibre, potassium and vitamin B12, which acts as a detoxifying agent. It has a low glycaemic index, which makes it excellent for diabetic patients. It is a great source of polyphenols and antioxidants, such as gentisic acid and ferolic acid, which help reduce inflammation in the body, reverse the ageing process, improve immunity, control blood sugar, reduce high blood pressure and accelerate weight loss. In fact, it helps dissolve kidney stones and is the perfect cure for diarrhoea and snake bites. The juice of the banana stem helps flush out toxins from the body. It is a diuretic, which aids bowel movement and contains good fibre for your gut.

Fermented probiotic drinks: The market is flooded with probiotics to aid digestion and metabolism. However, if you are a pitta (fire) dominant person with symptoms of excess heat, sweating, hyperacidity, reflux or burning sensations, then you must avoid fermented drinks. It can worsen the symptoms, trigger high metabolic fire and inflammation under the skin, and aggravate skin disorders like psoriasis, rosacea, eczema and urticaria.

Buttermilk: The best probiotic you can have post-meal is a diluted yoghurt drink. Traditionally, buttermilk is the liquid left behind after churning butter out of cultured cream, but salted lassi is also called buttermilk in many parts, and can be used as a daily drink. You can take two teaspoons of yoghurt, whip it well and add a glass of water to it. Add condiments like cumin powder and pink salt and garnish with cilantro. Buttermilk is cooling in nature, as the water prevents the bacteria from fermenting further. The bacteria found in yoghurt or curd ferment in the presence of heat, which is why, when you have just plain yoghurt or curd, it starts fermenting as soon as it comes into contact with the stomach heat, causing a burning sensation or symptoms of acidity.

Homemade protein drink

If you are working out regularly, you may need additional protein to replenish your body and build new tissues. But ensure that protein does not constitute more than one-third of your dietary intake and that it is consumed with equal portions of vegetables and carbohydrates. Most store-bought protein drinks are loaded with preservatives, which give them a longer shelf life. They can harm the gut, liver and kidneys in the long run due to improper digestion, aggregation of protein and elevated creatine levels. You can make your protein drink at home, which is fresh and easier to digest, absorb and assimilate. Take two teaspoons of roasted gram flour, which is your chickpea flour, add some dried fruits, cardamom and organic sweetener and boil in a glass of cruelty-free dairy or plant-based milk or just plain water. Consume this post-workout to rejuvenate your body. It is popularly known as *sattu* and is favoured by bodybuilders and traditional wrestlers in India.

All of this information may seem overwhelming in the beginning, but with repeated reading, you will be able to register it in your subconscious mind and eat in a more mindful way. Take baby steps, make one change at a time. Ever since I started sharing these food chemistry tips on social media, we gained half a million followers from ninety-seven countries within a fortnight. The algorithms worked in my favour, and I was able to share this with a diverse audience around the world. Within a few weeks, our inbox and comments were filled with messages from followers who shared their stories on how they had suffered severe gut health issues for over a decade and doctors couldn't find a cure for them. And by just following the food chemistry rules, they were able to heal gastritis, indigestion, reflux, GERD, IBS, constipation, anxiety, and symptoms of depression that had plagued them and affected the quality of a normal life.

Following is a quick summary of all the compatible and incompatible food combinations, that you can save on your phone or desktop for constant access. I wish someone had given me these tools when I was a teenager. But better late, than never . . .

FOOD GROUP COMBINATIONS		COMPATIBILITY
Fruits thumbrule : Eat it alone, or leave it alone		
Fruit with fruit	Incompatible	*Avoid mixing sweet, sour, astringent food groups in fruit salads. Eat one fruit group at a time.
Melons with other fruits, dairy, vegetables, grains	Toxic	Melons to be seperated from all food and fruit groups
Fruits with dairy based milk	Toxic	Fruit smoothie / milkshake / ice creams are toxic. Exception: mango, avacado can be mixed with milk (but not with yoghurt/ curd)
Fruits with plant based milk	Compatible	But leads to sluggish digestion
Fruits with yoghurt / curd	Toxic	Leads to fermentation and toxic byproducts in the gut
Fruit with cheese	Toxic	Leads to toxic by product, long term gut health and skin disorders
Fruit with nuts	Compatible	Comes from the same part of the plant
Fruits with warm spices	Healthy	Stew fruits with warm spices like cinnamon, cardamom, clove, pepper, star anise, to cure constipation and colon health issues
Fruits with sugar / honey	Incompatible	Fructose and sugar leads to fermentation in the gut
Fruits with vegetables	Incompatible	Fruit and vegetable mixed in a smoothie or a salad, impairs digestion, weakens the agni
Fruit with cereals, oats, grains	Incompatible	Impairs digestion, weakens the agni
Fruit stewed or cooked with grain	Avoid	Leads to sluggish digestion
Baked fruits / frozen fruit sorbets without mik	In moderation	When consumed in excess can weaken digestive health
Fruits with seeds	Avoid	Seeds must be pre soaked and added to warm foods or cooked with foods

*Note
(1) Sweet fruits like mangao, ripe banana, avacado, papaya, custard apple, wood apple can be had together
(2) Sour fruits like lemon, orange, tangerine, sour mango, sour grapes can be had together
(3) Astringent fruits like apples, berries, cherries, strawberries, pear can be had together

DAIRY AND PLANT BASED MILK		
Dairy / plant based milk with ghee or plant based butter	Healthy	Helps treat constipation and colon health issues
Dairy / plant based milk with nuts or spices	Compatible	Can add dried nuts, turmeric, pepper, cinnamon, clove, cardamom, ginger, star anise, nutmeg. Nuts must be presoaked overnight.
Dairy with vegetables	Incompatible	Exception: can add cottage or fresh cheese to cooked vegetable gravies, can cook carrots with milk, can boil garlic in milk for medicinal properties.
Plant based milk with vegetables	Compatible	Can add coconut milk to vegetable curries
Dairy with grains	Avoid	Leads to sluggish digestion
Dairy (milk / yoghurt / curd) with seafood, meat, eggs	Toxic	The metabolic by product can trigger skin disorders
Dairy with salty snacks	Toxic	Causes stomach cramps from the curdling process
DAIRY OR PLANT BASED YOGHURT AND CURD		
Yoghurt / curd with milk	Avoid	Impairs digestion and leads to gastritis
Yoghurt / curd with fruits	Toxic	Creates toxic by products, that ferment in the gut, and can trigger leaky gut syndrome.
Yoghur / curd with vegetables	Heed caution	Yoghurt can be mixed with carrot, cucumber, beetroot to make a dip. Add carminative spices like cumin, pink salt, curry leaf, dilute with water to aid digestion. Avoid adding sour foods like lemon, tomato, tamarind chutney in yoghurt or curd. Avoid night shade vegetables like tomato, potato, brinjal, and peppers.
Yoghurt / curd with cheese	Toxic	Yoghurt, curd and cheese are at different stages of metabolic process and can create metabolic waste when mixed together
Yoghurt / curd with other proteins like legumes (lentils, pulses, beans, peas), eggs, and tofu	Heed caution	Yoghurt or curd should not be mixed with other protein groups, as it can lead to severe indigestion, gases, bloating and diarrhoea.
Yoghur / curd with rice	Compatible	Staple meal when suffering from stomach issues. Add carminative spices like cumin, pink salt, curry leaf, chilly and water.

CHEESE		
Cheese with milk / yoghurt / fruit / beans / hot drinks / eggs	Toxic	Causes delay in digestion
VEGETABLES THUMBRULE - ALWAYS CHOOSE COOKED OVER RAW FOODS		
Vegetable juices	Avoid	Spinach and kale must NEVER be juiced / made into a smoothie, leads to kidney stones and impairs digestion. Exception for juicing - carrot, beetroot, bitter gourd with tomato, ashgourd, celery, cucumber, washed cilantro
Vegetables smoothies with milk / yoghurt / curd	Toxic	Exception: can add cottage or fresh cheese to cooked vegetable gravies, can cook carrots with milk, can boil garlic in milk for medicinal properties.
Raw vegetable salads	Unhealthy	Leafy green especially must not be consumed raw, as it impairs gut health. Blanch, steam, boil or cook all vegetables. Exception: carrot and cucumber can be consumed raw.
Steamed / boiled / blanched / cooked vegetables	Healthy	Suitable for all body types
Vegetable soups	Healthy	Suitable for all body types, seaons, topographic conditions
Vegetables with grains	Healthy	Presoak all grains, cook with vegetables and add warm carminative spices like cumin, fennel, coriander, garlic, ginger, asafoetida, and herbs like bay leaf, rosemary, thyme, basil
Vegetables with legumes (lentils, pulses, beans, peas), nuts and seeds	Compatible	Presoak all grains and cook with vegetables and carminative spices
Deep fried vegetables, fries, potato chips	Toxic	Releases acrylamide, destroys nutrients
GRAINS THUMBRULE - PRESOAK ALL GRAINS, LEGUMES (LENTILS, PULSES, BEANS, PEAS) FOR 4-12 HOURS		
Grains with nuts / seeds	Compatible	Ensure to presoak all before cooking
Grains with fruits / dairy	Incompatible	
Grains with Tapioca	Avoid	starch with grains can trigger bloating, stomach pain, gas, nausea

OTHER INCOMPATIBLE COMBINATIONS		
Heated honey	Toxic	Releases HMF. Temperatue should be below 42 degree celcius
Honey in hot beverages, baked cookies, cakes, cereals	Toxic	Releases HMF
Honey in dairy / plant based milk	Compatible	Ensure to not cook honey
Honey on fruits	Compatible	But leads to sugar spike
Honey with yoghurt / curd	Compatible	Helps ground and reduce nervouness, anxiety
Lemon and cucumber	Incompatible	Contradictory properties
Protein with fats and starch	Incompatible	Causes delay in digestion
Protein with other proteins	Incompatible	Causes delay in digestion

11

Seven Tools That Helped Shape My Life . . . and Gut Health

As a child, I was fortunate enough to be exposed to different religions. I was born into a Jain family and learned the scriptures at a young age. I spent quality time with the female monks who would visit my neighbourhood. In school, I was exposed to the Vedic texts and learned the Bhagavad Gita, Vishnu Sahastranamam and Aditya Hridayam. On Fridays, we would read verses from the Quran. For high school, I went to a convent, where I visited the chapel every morning and Sister Theresa would read from the Bible. Over the years, I continued to visit her. I was the last person she spoke to, after which she went into a prayer state for two days and passed on. She took my pain with her. During my travels, I visited all the gurudwaras and Buddhist monasteries I crossed.

When I started researching Ayurveda, I found many similarities between this science and spirituality. Ayurveda states that the four purposes of life are: 1) *Dharma*, following the path of righteousness; 2) *Artha*, earning money in a legal way; 3) *Kama*, fulfilling all your desires without causing harm to another; and 4) *Moksha*, breaking the cycle of life and death to attain salvation. Health is spiritual. When the natural sciences help cure the diseases in your body, they are preparing you.

Ayurveda and yoga prepare
your body for meditation, so you attain salvation.

Remember, your gut flora impacts your mental and emotional health.

Your gut stores emotions and memories; your GI tract is sensitive to emotions; and your intuition comes from the gut. Similarly, your state of mind also impacts your gut. When you are stressed in your personal life, your gut health also gets impaired. When your personal and professional lives are in good shape, your gut health also improves.

Once, my friend Wendy and I were talking until 2 a.m. Our conversation went on for four hours, during which we spoke about things that gave us joy—about spirituality, reincarnation, and finding our purpose in life; we shared our deepest secrets and truths. They were surreal hours when the time felt like it had frozen. Wendy was in the last stage of ovarian cancer and had a medical condition where litres of fluid would collect in her stomach and she needed to visit a hospital to get it drained using intrusive medical pipes. But after our Zoom call, all that happiness caused Wendy to experience a natural release of those fluids. Such is the impact of the mind on your gut.

Here are the seven tools that helped me heal my emotions and my gut health and shaped my life.

1. Break up with your past

You may have heard these sayings: 'History repeats itself', 'It runs in the family' and 'It is a hereditary disease.' Well, the theory is true. But you are still in the driver's seat and in control of your destination. You will become what you eat; your inner circle of seven friends will determine your mental makeup; the content you consume will become your thought process; and your thoughts will become your reality.

If you continue living and eating as your parents and grandparents did, you will end up with the same health problems or diseases as they did. Calling it a hereditary disease is just an excuse we make—to avoid taking action, to avoid making radical changes to our diets and lifestyles, to avoid giving up our comfort foods and vices.

Diseases have a psychosomatic origin. Often, our childhood memories and trauma manifest in the form of diseases as we grow up. I am sorry if you had a terrible childhood. I am sorry if your parents were awful to you for no reason or projected their hate and childhood trauma on to you. I am truly sorry for you, and I feel for you. But listen, this is no reason for you to continue suffering.

Perhaps your parents didn't have healthy eating habits; maybe they didn't have a supportive environment and suppressed their emotions; maybe they didn't heal from their childhood trauma. But that is no reason for you to carry forward their emotional baggage and project generations of trauma onto your children. The buck stops with you. The abuse ends here. The toxic patterns end now. By taking action and making radical changes, you choose to start the healing process.

Recognize the toxicity that affects you; name it, label it, and journal all those negative emotions that made you choose bad relationships, eat unhealthily or abuse your body. Make a resolution to heal those memories and release them from your body. Choose to change.

Exercise the power of choice.

To be a lotus that grows despite the muck,
To be a lighthouse that ships come home to,
To be a beacon of hope for future generations.

Have you heard of the 95:5 rule? Say you are dealing with heartbreak or stress at work or in your family life. The event itself amounts to only 5 per cent of the problem; 95 per cent of it is your reaction. You have given so much energy and power to your problem by constantly thinking about it that it has grown from the size of a mustard seed to a mountain. It is now exaggerated in your mind and is growing like a tumour in your body. It is feeding on all your good energy, vibrations and thoughts, growing quickly and destroying you from within.

What can you do? Reorient your reaction to it.

Move away from problem-thinking to problem-solving.

Analyse the problem and make a list of possible solutions. List all permutations and combinations until you arrive at the perfect solution. This is a far more constructive way of handling things. Remember to remove your emotions from the brainstorming process as well. Do not think with your mind or heart. Instead, think from your gut, apply your heart to your decision and execute it with your mind. While your brain is rational and analyses information, intuition comes from your gut and empathy comes from your heart. Take this road to holistic wellness so you can heal your body, mind and emotions. Anxiety is like quicksand. If you struggle, you will sink faster and it will consume you. But if you stay still and motionless, you will float. You have to let the moment pass and stop reacting to it.

God lives in the details

When you find yourself getting anxious, restless, or overthinking things, simply step back and look at one of God's creations; the smaller, the better. It could be a flower, a leaf or even an ant. Observe how marvellous and beautiful this creation is. Perfect colour, anatomy, symmetry and texture. So many miracles of this universe are packed into one little creation. Just looking at it for a few minutes will ground you, humble you about your presence in this world and reduce your anxiety.

2. Meditate

Your mind is like a canvas. On any given day, we have over 60,000 thoughts in our minds, the majority of which are unnecessary and useless to us. They are simply noise and clutter in your brain. You need to create an empty white space on this canvas to introduce new ideas, thoughts and colours to your life.

Set an alarm for 4.45 a.m. and get out of bed by at least 5.15 a.m. (I like to hit the snooze button too on some days!) Freshen up and put on some comfortable white cotton clothes. Use the same outfit for meditation and set it aside exclusively for this ritual, as it holds all your good energy and vibrations. Place your fingers gently in the middle of your forehead. This is where your intellectual capacity comes from. This is the third eye. Close your eyes and focus on your breath. Gently inhale and exhale, creating an empty, white space in the middle of your forehead. Let it grow and expand, with each breathtaking over your mind, body and soul. Let this white cloud envelop you and cradle you in its healing properties. Meditate for five, ten, twenty or sixty minutes, as long as you can. But start. I also love to chant because it helps set the vibration for the day through sound waves. Chanting also helps replace any negative sounds and thoughts in our minds with positive sounds and vibrations.

3. Practice manifesting and gratitude

Manifesting is a powerful tool, but you must do it right so you don't end up feeling frustrated or defeated. Manifesting is like going to a restaurant. You need to be clear about what you want to order from that restaurant, from this universe. There is an abundance of health, happiness, prosperity, success, healthy relationships, goodness, gratitude, forgiveness, modesty and all those beautiful positive emotions. But there is also an abundance of negative emotions. You have to choose what you want to receive. Do you want to have that healthy food or that junk snack? Do you want to experience positive emotions or negative emotions? You have to choose what you want to experience and the universe will serve it to you.

Do not complete any negative sentence in your mind or in your words. Whenever you have a negative thought, say 'cancel, cancel, cancel' three times loudly! Your brain will immediately stop. It will become a habit to cancel negative thoughts. Immediately replace that sentence or thought with a positive, constructive one, like, 'I am healthy, I am strong, I am happy'. The universe doesn't hear your words. It simply responds to your vibration, positive or negative, and you attract events based on the frequency at which you are vibrating. When you say, 'I don't want to be sad,' the universe just responds to the negative vibration of the word 'sad' and gives you more sadness, and you don't need that! So ask for what you want. Be very clear, precise and positive.

Once you've ordered, be patient. Don't follow the chef around or nag the universe over and over.

Manifest what you want, and let it go!

Words are powerful; they become your reality. Say these words in your mind: 'May I speak the truth, and may what I speak become the truth. May my manifestations become my reality. May I become the kalpavriksh (wish-fulfilling divine tree) of my own body and manifest what I want.'

And do not manifest with expectations, because the gap between your reality and your expectations will only lead to frustration. That's an unhappy equation. Instead:

Manifest and marry it with gratitude.

Place your fingers gently on both eyes and express gratitude to the universe for everything that you've received to date. You are the sum of all the magical events that have happened in this universe for you to become who you are right now. Remember this magical thought:

You are within the universe,
and the entire Universe is within you.

Any time there is a scarcity in life, the universe fills it up with another opportunity. It is up to us to see that the glass is half-full. Hardships in life are also opportunities that challenge us to grow to our fullest potential. I wouldn't be who I am if it weren't for the good and bad moments that shaped my journey. And I count my blessings each waking day. Because:

Being alive is the greatest gift we receive every
single morning.

There are so many people in this world who may have passed quietly in their sleep and did not wake up to see the sunrise today. You were gifted another day to live your dreams, to create a positive impact on this planet and to tell your loved ones how much you love them. Gratitude is a wonderful exercise and the universe loves gratitude. When you're grateful for what you already have—a healthy body, a loving family, food on your plate, a roof over your head, a loyal friend and a whole lot of other things— you will attract more events to be grateful for. Gratitude allows you to embrace what you have and experience contentment, peace and happiness. By feeling grateful, you are basically telling the Universe what you want to continue feeling.

Science says that gratitude is one of the most powerful emotions we can experience. It vibrates at 540 MHZ, which is the highest possible frequency your body can experience and is the same as love.

When you dial into the frequency of gratitude,
you become a co-creator of this universe!

Here is another powerful secret: When you vibrate energy into the universe, it comes right back at you like a boomerang. But the universe also multiplies this energy before sending it back, be it a positive or negative emotion. So, be careful what you vibrate.

4. Realize the power of forgiveness

One of the most powerful tools we have been given is the power to forgive. This small exercise could help you offload so much baggage from your mind, heart and gut.

Write down the name of the person who is bothering you right now, who has hurt you, broken your heart, cheated you and shaken your faith and confidence in yourself and humanity. Write down the name of that person, because it is time to set them free. They don't deserve to live rent-free in your head and your heart and dictate how you feel throughout the day. It is time to set them free and to set yourself free. It is also time to forgive yourself for what you went through and stop punishing yourself for their mistakes.

Remember, this heart and body are like a cup. You have to empty the negative emotions so you can create space to receive positive emotions like love, kindness, empathy, forgiveness and compassion in your life, which you deserve. A broken heart is only going to attract more broken people into your life. A kind and healed heart will attract more kind people into your life. And the minute you release those negative thoughts and memories, your gut also releases those negative emotions that are stored there. It makes room for healthy food and healthy memories. Your appetite, metabolism, gut health and mental and emotional health start improving. Forgive them, because you deserve to witness the kindest version of yourself and the world deserves it too.

To err is humanity. To forgive is divinity.

Forgive your parents. The most important struggle I have seen in many of my patients and friends—and I faced this too—was letting go of our childhood disappointments. In India, there is a proverb that goes, 'It takes seven lifetimes to repay the debt to your parents for giving birth to you and allowing you this human experience'. This is what you can do for your parents in return. Forgive them for any mistakes they may have made during your childhood or adulthood. Remember, they are also human beings going through this world of experiences. Take care of their health even more now because they've entered the degenerative stage of their lives (also called the vata phase in Ayurveda), where their bones, muscles, and tissues are emaciating rapidly. There are Ayurvedic treatments such as *janu basti, kati basti* and *greva basti*, which involve pooling medicated oil on their knees, lower back and neck. This helps strengthen their joints and muscles. There is a powerful treatment called *hridaya basti* that helped a patient recover from blocked arteries. The treatment involves placing a mould around the chest region and gently pouring medicated oil into the mould, which creates a gentle rhythm around the heart region and stimulates blood flow. The body, in response to this help opens up another artery to compensate for the blocked artery. When you give your body the right therapy, it can heal itself. There are also treatments such as *navarakizhi*, which is a poultice massage with medicated rice, milk and herbs, to strengthen muscles. Several Ayurvedic medicines such as *gandha thailam, avipati choornam* and *manasamitra vatakam* help take care of symptoms like low bone density, insomnia and chronic constipation. Please note that all Ayurvedic medicines must be administered only after consulting with an Ayurvedic doctor. Take them to an Ayurvedic doctor and give them the gift of good health.

Most importantly, be a part of your parents' spiritual journey. They are at a stage where having completed all their duties towards their children, they are looking for answers to their lives. If they want to visit a church, temple, mosque, or even take a nature walk, please accompany them or help them in their efforts. In Kashi, I saw an old-age home where people come to stay during their last days to embrace death and God gracefully. In Jainism, people in their conscious state choose to give up food and water, family and all worldly attachments and enter a meditative, self-realization stage, also called *santara* or samadhi.

5. Practice unconditional love

The truest form of love is love without conditions or expectations. Love someone so deeply that you won't even need to tell them how you feel. But expect nothing in return. Your ability to love is your greatest gift. Because when that love blossoms like a garden in your heart, it is you who enjoys the gifts—the chirping of the birds, the dewy soft grass under your feet, the fragrance of those flowers and the pure joy of being alive. Love vibrates at the highest possible frequency that a human body can experience.

This Indian proverb best captures the depth of the feeling of love in our hearts.

पोथी पढ़ि पढ़ि जग मुआ, पंडित भया न कोय।
ढाई आखर प्रेम का, पढ़े सो पंडित होय।।

Nobody becomes knowledgeable just by acquiring
bookish knowledge.
Knowledge is love. One who has embraced love
becomes knowledgeable.

Love without expectations. Don't project your expectations onto other people and expect them to fulfil your needs. You can't give in to their physical needs and expect them to fill your cup with mental and emotional support. Love is not a transaction. That is unfair. Love is kind, nurturing, and caring; love is silent; love is a sacrifice, as per an African proverb. But lust is loud, taking and breaking hearts, and that's not who you are. You are unconditional love.

Remember, love for the physical body is nothing but a validation and expression of that emotional love. Your mental and emotional selves do not care for that. It only needs kindness, compassion, empathy and forgiveness. Your spiritual body is above all of that. It is complete by itself and needs nothing more. Because your spiritual body is pure love. It is part of your God as much as it is part of my God.

And before you love another person, remember to fill your cup and your heart with self-love and unconditional kindness towards yourself. One way to do this is to embrace the child inside you.

Someone once said to me, 'I am in too much pain; what can I do?'

I replied, 'Do you want to know what happened? You have forgotten the child inside of you. Tell me, when was the last time you did something new for the first time?' Have you seen the joy and wonder on a child's face when they do something new, like making their first soapy bubble, spotting a puppy-shaped cloud in the sky, building a sandcastle, or even getting wet in the rain? As we grow up, we forget these simple joys in our lives. We are busy paying bills and taxes, fighting with family over property and money, building toxic bridges with our siblings and our friends, calculating every single love move and drawing territories around ourselves, which become smaller by the day. As a result, we shrink. We forget who we are. Don't forget that innocent, pure child inside of you.

Don't live in the future and worry about it, because it is nothing but a figment of your imagination. Tomorrow doesn't exist. It is never going to come. Live in the present moment. Make it count. Make it a beautiful moment that you can cherish. Because, at the end of your life, no one is going to remember how much money you made. But they will remember the memories you created with them. Make your moments count and live like it is your last day on earth with no regrets or unfinished jobs. Nothing but pure love for yourself and those around you. Embrace the child inside of you so you can live a healthy and joyous life.

6. Finding *Ikigai*

Ikigai is a Japanese concept that means finding purpose in your life and a reason for living. It urges you to explore your consciousness, heart and soul: what are you good at, what are you passionate about, what does the world need right now and can the world pay for this service of yours?

I found my Ikigai in this profession, but I also look for Ikigai in my daily choices. Engage in deeper dialogues with yourself when doing any small tasks, like ordering food or buying a new dress. Do I need this? Does it add value to my life? Does this negatively impact my environment and ecosystem? We humans are the only sentient beings that create no value for this planet. We only consume. The least we can do is make more mindful choices in our daily lives.

Less is more. This is another Japanese concept based on the concept of minimalism, where you embrace simplicity and let go of clutter, noise and unnecessary things in your life. The problem with desire is that it is a never-ending cycle. It is like a bottomless pit. You will never have enough. In fact, gluttony and greed are considered sins in many spiritual practices.

So, how can we break this pattern? If you are hungry and have an appetite for three pieces of bread, have just two pieces. Instead of having five items on your plate, choose to have only four or maybe three. Sit back and wait a few minutes for your stomach to communicate to the brain that you are indeed content. Allow some space for the digestive juices and stomach acids to digest the food, absorb it and assimilate the nutrients. Don't overload the gut–brain axis such that it stops communicating with you.

The same rule applies to relationships and your home. Give space to your partner and allow the relationship to flourish.

Declutter your home so the positive energy can move around freely.

When you consume less, think less and react less,
You create space for more!

7. Be kind

Being strong is easy. But to be kind, despite any hardships you might have faced, shows real strength of character. Be kind. To yourself and everyone around you. Hold no bias or judgement. Place your hands on your heart chakra and pray that every word, thought, action, or deed that comes out of you is filled with kindness, compassion, forgiveness, empathy and love.

Don't say anything mean to anyone, because you do not know how much pain they may be hiding behind their smile. And if you have something kind to say, don't waste another minute— just say it. Life is short. Life is unpredictable. Say something kind to the people you love, say something kind to the people you do not love, and most importantly, say something kind to the people you do not know how to love. Your kindness could change that person's perception of the world and their pain. Your one act of kindness can save someone's life and stop them from ending it.

Speak only if you have something kind to say.

Embrace the differences between us. No matter what roles you play in your life, kindness must flow freely from your heart, like a river nourishing everyone in its path. It must flow freely, without bias, to everyone—irrespective of their religion, caste, community, creed, race, skin colour, hierarchy, nationality or gender orientation.

In fact, children can teach us the true act of kindness. Did you know that God walks on earth—as children? They have such divinity on their faces and unconditional kindness and happiness in their innocent hearts, which is worth protecting and fighting for. What can we do for them?

Dear parents, don't project your unfinished or broken dreams onto your child. It's not their job to fulfil your dreams. They are souls born to realize their dreams and journeys. They only come through you; they don't belong to you. Don't project your trauma onto the child, because the child stores trauma in the body, which manifests in the form of diseases. Any kind of emotional damage done during their formative years will stay with them for years and take several more years to reverse.

Put on your child's plate freshly cooked foods that are loaded with prana—the source of life. Choose foods with high-vibrational frequencies, such as fruits, vegetables, grains, pulses, legumes, lentils, nuts and seeds. Don't put junk on the plate, processed foods, overcooked foods, or even meat and seafood. It's not fair to put the child of another entity on your child's plate. It's not fair to either of them. Make sure to introduce Ayurvedic herbs into their diet at an early age and educate them on the combinations of foods to eat and avoid. Remember, your child depends on you to make the right decisions in their life.

Sometimes, I meet young children in the clinic who are confused about their gender. Puberty hits, and there is chaos and conflict in the body because the body is going in one direction and the child is not mentally prepared for it. This can trigger anxiety, stress, clinical depression and even suicidal tendencies.

There are some remedies in Ayurveda that help reduce the anxiety and stress that come from these hormonal imbalances. *Shirodhara* is a process where warm medicated oils are gently dripped on the middle of the forehead in a rhythmic manner to stimulate the pituitary gland and reduce cortisol. *Nasyam*—introducing medicated oil drops through the nostrils—also helps stimulate the pituitary gland and reduce hormonal imbalances. Note, these treatments cannot change a person's gender orientation. We cannot change that and should not try to change it. We can only reduce the anxiety that comes from it.

Most importantly, remember that:

The spirit has no gender.

The spirit is neither male nor female. And in several cultures, such as the Native American community and Asian community, all five genders are recognized—male with a male personality, female with a female personality, male with a female personality, female with a male personality, and one with both personalities.

Gender orientation is not a disease.
Addiction to sex is a disease.

We need to learn how to be kind to each other. Humanity fails when we use hatred to defeat hatred.

I have witnessed the men in my family suffer and pay a heavy price for their inability to express themselves. Men should have the space to share their pain, their struggles, their vulnerabilities, their tears and their trauma as well. Sadly, many traditional societies project lofty expectations on young boys, expecting them to carry the family legacy and businesses forward at the cost of their dreams. Dear men, you have both the X and Y chromosomes. You have in you both masculine and feminine energies. The male energy protects and provides; the feminine energy nourishes. When you embrace the two, you're in a state of kindness, happiness and health. But when there is a conflict between the two, it leads to toxic masculinity and diseases and disorder at the physical, mental, emotional, energetic and spiritual levels. We need you to take care of yourselves. Don't wait until it's too late. And:

Don't sacrifice parts of your health to make wealth for your family.

Because when you get sick, it affects not only you but your loved ones too. Ayurveda offers treatments such as shirodhara and abhyangam to reduce physical and mental stress and medicines such as *ashokarishtam* and *ashwagandharishtam* that help boost male fertility and health.

Most importantly, respect the portal through which you came to this world. Every time you hurt a woman, you are hurting the co-creator of this universe.

And be kind to animals. They experience complex emotions and pain too. Mother earth cries at the cruelty faced by her creations. In fact, there is a new theory[*] that says the continuous butchering of thousands of animals, for several years, generates acoustic anisotropy, or pain waves, that can trigger earthquakes. We already know that sound waves put great stress on rocks. Even water stores negative and positive energies. So where does the negative energy from slaughtered animals go? The Einsteinian Pain Waves (EPW) theory explains that while primary and secondary waves move quickly, pain waves build up pressure over a period of time. And when they reach a flash point, the crust of the earth breaks and reacts in the form of an earthquake. This is discussed with compelling research in the book *Etiology*

---

[*] Maneka Gandhi, 'Measuring Collective Pain', *The Statesman*, March 3, 2019, https://www.thestatesman.com/supplements/8thday/measuring-collective-pain-1502714915.html, accessed on June 8, 2023.

of Earthquakes: A New Approach, written by Madan Mohan Bajaj and his colleagues, who also explain that the EPW travel a great distance with time and that slaughterhouses in one country can lead to havoc in another country. It is the butterfly effect all over again.

Animals contribute greatly to farming and humanity. In an incident in 1984, a tragic gas leak in Bhopal killed more than 20,000 people. But statistics showed that people living in houses with walls coated in cow dung were not as affected because the organic coating absorbed much of the toxic leak.

We all come from earth and go back to earth. Our human bodies and all the animals and plants are made of this earth. Be kind to mother earth. We have done much damage to the rhythm of the planet and caused such a tragic change in the climate that our children are paying the price. The air is not breathable, the water is not drinkable, the oceans are filled with plastic and bleed red from all that whale hunting, there are unseasonal rains and flash floods and coastal cities are slowly sinking.

It's also important to be kind to yourself and learn how to express your feelings. Screaming and shouting, fighting and crying are not ways of expressing yourself. They can trigger imbalances in your throat chakra, lead to overproduction or underproduction of the thyroid hormone and cause diseases.

What can you do? First, at a mental and emotional level, you must learn how to express yourself. Have some clarity in your mind and write down what you want to express to the other person. Read it again to make sure there is no emotional toxicity or blame game in it. Rather, it is a clear expression of your thoughts.

Next, when you are speaking to that person who may have hurt you, express yourself freely and confidently. But do not project your emotional damage onto that person. Express yourself without blaming the other person for what you are feeling.

And most importantly, keep your end goal in mind. What are you trying to achieve? Is it an amicable solution? Is it an apology? Or are you trying to nurture and repair this relationship? Physical scars and diseases can be healed, but mental and emotional scars from words that we have spoken can take years to fade. Don't speak in haste, so you don't have to experience guilt and regret later.

What can we do for ourselves and those around us? Ground yourself and regulate your emotions from time to time. There is a variety of emotions that we go through from day to day. Success is one of the most corrupt emotions that can create an inflated ego in our minds and you have to have more and more success to feed that ego. This doesn't allow you to experience the smaller joys in life. Don't let success go to your head. Enjoy that accomplishment for 120 seconds, then immediately ground yourself. It's a simple 120-second rule that you must follow for all emotions, be they joy or sadness.

Don't let jealousy and envy enter your heart, because your heart is where the garden of love blossoms. Don't let negative emotions corrupt that garden. And don't let junk and unhealthy food enter your body. Especially dead foods, like meat and seafood, that have no prana, the source of life in them. Animals release cortisol, a stress hormone at the time of confinement, torture and slaughter. Where does that cortisol go when you eat that meat? It goes into your body and triggers imbalances and more complex diseases of the mind and body.

And when sadness comes into your life, embrace it with the same dignity, humility and grace as you did with happiness. Because that sadness has come into your life to teach you an important lesson. Don't give up hope. After every dark night, there is a sunrise. And when the dark clouds have exhausted their raindrops and tears on you, there is going to be sunshine and a rainbow on the other side. And you have to be there to see that. So don't give up.

God, nature and your parents gave you this body to go through this world of human experiences. So, you can evolve and become the kindest and healthiest version of yourself. Don't give up.

In Ayurveda, there are a series of therapies that help cure depression. Treatments such as shirodhara and nasyam help stimulate the pituitary gland and release serotonin in the body. Ayurvedic medicines like saraswatarishtam and *manasamitra vatakam* help cure anxiety, insomnia and even post-partum depression. There is also *shiro-pichu* treatment, which helps reduce anxiety and depression in children. Once, a nurse from California came to us to treat her clinical depression. She was taking eight anti-depressant pills a day. Within just a few days of intense panchakarma treatment, where toxins were removed from her body, she was able to reduce her medicine intake by half. And soon after, she was able to completely stop those anti-depressants because she was naturally happy from within.

Forest bathing

When you visit an Ayurvedic retreat in the Western Ghats in India, you will often find it located amidst natural elements like tall trees, local flora and fauna, backwaters or even facing a river. Spending time in nature has many mental, physical and spiritual health benefits. It is a powerful antidote to the pressures of the modern world and is based on thousands of years of intuitive knowledge—that we are part of nature and we must reconnect with nature from time to time. It helps reduce the production of the stress hormone, lowers heart rate and blood pressure, boosts the immune system, accelerates recovery from illness, improves feelings of happiness and stimulates creativity. In fact, Japan has a similar concept of forest bathing called *shinrin yoku,* which simply means spending time in nature.

Above all, practise making space for yourself and marking healthy boundaries. Don't allow anyone to project their toxicity onto you, or to show disrespect to your body, mind, emotions, virtues, values or spiritual journey. Be kind and unapologetically you.

Be kind to yourself
because the world needs you.

Epilogue

Ayurveda helped me heal my body, mind and emotions. But there were other modalities too. I read various religious scriptures for answers, learned sailing, surfing, travelled to many countries in search of answers, worked hard at the gym and yoga studios, trained with horses, became a certified yoga instructor, tried *kalarippayattu* and *qi gong*, signed up for therapy, got cranium sacral, *Tera-Mieseiche*, theta healing, hypnotherapy and access bar sessions done. I kept hoping to get better, not knowing I had to do the work myself.

Don't be so busy in this world that you have no time for yourself. Take a moment, to listen to your body, to feel your emotions, to heal your broken parts and to learn to cherish those scars that you have earned like a tiger or a tigress. Don't hide them, but wear them with pride. Give all of your heart, mind, and soul to your healing journey. Be both disciplined and kind, because you deserve to experience the healthiest and kindest version of yourself and the world deserves it too.

* * *

If you have made it to this page, I thank you for being kind to yourself and for taking the time to read about the many ways in which we can heal ourselves. The purpose of writing this book was to share with you all the insights and knowledge I have had the opportunity to gather during my personal journey and through my work at the clinic. Every time I watched patients heal, walk, run and smile again, it helped me heal as a person emotionally, mentally, and physically. I witnessed small and big miracles in my clinic every single day. I saw young multiple sclerosis patients walk again for the first time without physical support since the onset of their disease; we heard paralysis patients speak for the first time since their stroke; patients healing their intra-ocular pressure and retina even for which there is no cure, dissolving kidney stones and gall bladder stones; shrinking cysts and fibroids and avoiding surgeries. My wish is to prevent others from going through what I endured in my formative years due to a lack of knowledge. With this book, the clinic and the academy, my wish is to help you improve your health and live a more powerful life now, and that you can be there for your family, nurture yourself, sweeten your relationships, and enjoy the true joys of this universe.

I learned some beautiful words in Kashi.

Kashi means 'end of desire'. Human desires are endless, like a bottomless pit, and there will never be enough. You have to decide when and how much is enough for you.

Anitya, impermanence. It is a phenomenon in life that everything comes to an end and that nothing lasts forever. Both joy and grief.

Moksha, liberation. This is the only permanent truth. That you have the choice and power to liberate yourself from the cycle of life and death, joy and grief, disease and cure, highs and lows.

Let go of what doesn't serve you anymore. Keep letting go until you reach a permanent state of peace.

Wishing that you find the peace within you.

The truest form of love is self-love.
The best relationship, is the one with yourself
The only person who can heal you is you
Embrace your inner strength and rise
Release the generations of trauma you have carried
Shed the thorns that have become spikes in your flesh
Release those who have hurt you
Remember the forgotten parts and set them free
Embrace the innocent child inside of you
Make room for new memories and for love
And give yourself permission to heal
You deserve to witness the healthiest and kindest version
of yourself.
The world deserves it too.

Acknowledgements

To Deepthi, Yash, and the entire team at Penguin Random House India, Nityanand Prabhuji, and my literary agent for believing in me.

My enthusiastic passion force behind Prana.

The patients at Prana, my students and my virtual family for giving me an Ikigai, a reason to work harder.

Scan QR code to access the
Penguin Random House India website

Meditation Hall at my residence, Madanapalle

*With dear friends
Kathyayini Ratan
and Deepak Ratan*

With Federico Grandi at the release of Jewel in the Lotus *in
Spanish at Beunes Aires, Argentina*

Photographs courtesy Sri M.

With Sri Krishnadas Ji

With the sadhu samaj at the Purna Kumbh Mela, Haridwar, 2010

The Golden Temple Amritsar

With His Highness Marthanda Varma of Travancore at the talks in Thiruvananthapuram

With Dr Karan Singh at his residence

Trip to Kailash: The Kargyupa Buddhist Monastery at Saga

View of the Holy Kailash mountain

The Taj Mahal Hotel, Mumbai where Babaji appeared as a Sikh

Trip to Kailash, Guru Purnima at Saga

Trip to Kailash, at Yama Dwar
(entrance to the Kailash Parikrama)

At the lake near
Peepal Grove
School, Sadum

At the retreat in the Peepal Grove School
(l-r, Ajay, Kaizer, Geeta, Radhika, Shobha, Anjali, Abhijit, Sridharr)

With dear friends at my residence, Madanapalle
(l-r, Dr Vijaynarayana Reddy, Mohan Kumar, Surya Deo, Jyoti
Narang, Kirana Reddy, Sobha Reddy and Prabha Reddy)

With Head Mistress and students of Satsang Vidyalaya

Sunanda and I with the then President of India, Dr A. P. J. Abdul Kalam
Justice Venkatchellaiah and Dr Ajay Kumar Singh, at
the Peepal Grove School, Sadum

With students of the Satsang Vidyalaya at its inception

With Joseph Mar Ireneus, presently Joseph Mar Thoma, the Metropolitan of the Mar Thoma Syrian Church, at the United Nations Conference of Religious Leaders, New York, 2000.

With head of the Brahmakumaris at the United Nations Conference of religious leaders

With friend Jerry Jones in Portland, USA

Talk at Bharatiya Vidya Bhavan, Bangalore

Talk at Portland, USA

*With my dear classmates in Thiruvananthapuram
(l-r, Ranjit Sadasivan, Dr Narayana Prasad)*

*With my dear friends Sri Ramaswamy Pillai and neurologist
Dr Marthanda Pillai*

Bhagirathi peaks

*River Ganga descends at
Suryakund, Gangotri*

*Satsang at Vyas Guha, Mana beyond Badrinath
(far left, Pradeep, towards right, Viraj and Balaji)*

At the Grand Canyon, first visit to the USA

Painting for a friend in Germany

At a café near Frieburg Cathedral, Germany

In Ardha matsyendrasana at Rishikesh

River Ganga in Rishikesh

Gomukh, birthplace of the River Ganga

Seashore at Kanyakumari where Maayi Maa lived

River Ganga near Cheerbasa

At Charanpaduka behind Badrinath temple

Arundathi cave near Vashistha Guha

Cave at Maruthuvamalai, near Kanyakumari

Naina Swami

Swami Purushothamananda

Snow-clad Kedar range

Swami Tapasyananda, senior monk of the Ramakrishna order

Neem Karoli Baba of Kainchi, Almora

Sri Jiddu Krishnamurty

Swami Chidananda of the Divine Life Society, Rishikesh

Ramana Maharshi with a good friend

Sri Shyama Charan Lahiri, the great yogi, disciple of Sri Guru Babaji

*Nityananda Avadoota of
Ganeshpuri at a young age*

Maayi Maa, saint of Kanyakumari

Sri Ramakrishna Paramahamsa

*Swami Vivekananda as an
itinerant monk*

Sri Narayana Guru

Swami Abhedhananda

Sai Baba of Shirdi

Sri Chattambi Swami

Sri Gopalaswamy

Sri Kaladi Masthan

Poonthura Swamy

With Sunanda, her parents, brother and our children

Badrinath Temple

Kedarnath Temple

Sunanda and I before marriage

With family at Tunganath (l-r) Roshan, M, Sunanda, Aisha

My school – Government Model High School, Thycaud, Thiruvananthapuram

Tomb of Peer Mohammed Sahib, Thuckalay, Tamil Nadu

House in Vanchiyoor where I lived till the age of 14

Padmanabha Swamy temple and the sacred pond, Thiruvananthapuram

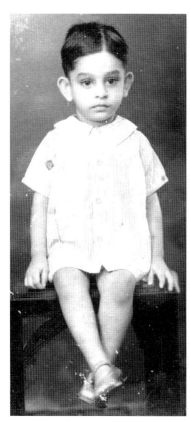

At three years of age

Reading Aristotle at 16

My two sisters

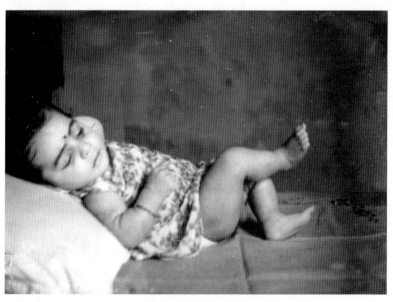

At six months

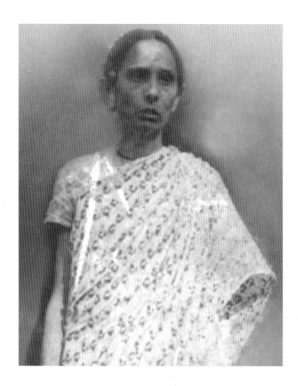

*My maternal
grandmother*

My father and mother

My Guru, Sri Maheshwarnath Babaji

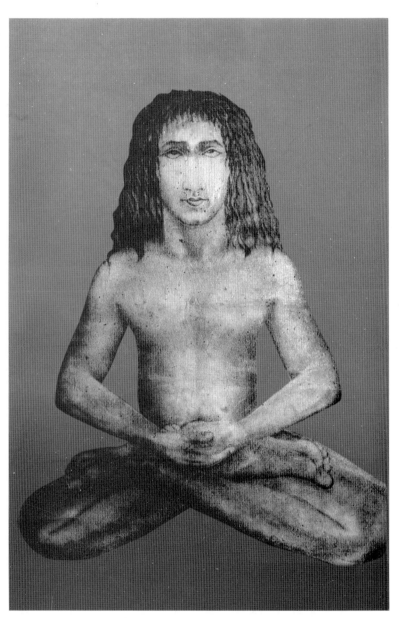

Sri Maheshwarnath's Guru, Sri Guru Babaji